Everything You Need To Know About Going To University

Sally Longson

KOGAN
PAGE

London • Stirling (USA)

First published in 1997

Kogan Page Limited
120 Pentonville Road
London N1 9JN
and
22883 Quicksilver Drive
Stirling, VA 20166, USA

© Sally Longson, 1997

British Library Cataloguing in Publication Data

A CIP record for this book is available from the British Library.

ISBN 0 7494 2222 X

Typeset by Kogan Page Ltd
Printed and bound in Great Britain by Clays Ltd, St Ives plc

Contents

Preface

Going on to higher education needs careful planning today. Although there is an increasing demand for graduates and salaries are rising accordingly, it's an option that cannot be regarded lightly. For a start, there is a wide range of courses and institutions to choose from, an increasing number of students going on to higher education ('Will a degree make that much difference?'), and financial worries. Plus, increasingly, employers expect to see that you have used your university days wisely and really *done* something with them. This all adds up to a lot of pressure. Research, think and plan ahead. It will make the journey through higher education all the more rewarding.

You will – inevitably – end up in debt. *Consider your university course to be an investment.* Most investments involve an initial cost before the rewards are gained. This does mean, however, that you owe it to yourself to think more carefully about what you want from the entire university experience including vacations. So that, when your prospective employer leans forward and asks you, 'Well, tell me, what did your university education do for you?' you know exactly what to say and know what you have to offer.

A word of warning: the higher education system is constantly evolving and will do so even faster. It must, if it is to meet the needs of all its customers. So make sure that all your advice is absolutely up to date. Watch for mention of top-up fees, changes to tuition fees, loans and grants, etc. It's your future and therefore your responsibility – but the good news is that there's plenty of help at hand.

Today, you can pave your own career path. The rules are rapidly disappearing and the route is up to you in so many areas. Whether you go to university or not, I wish you well. At the end of the day, the important thing is to be healthy and happy.

Good luck!

Please note!

Throughout this book, to save you from never-ending references to he/she, his/her etc, you'll see more often than not 'he' and 'his'. Women are as welcome as men into higher education but it will save you from constant repetition. Similarly, 'institution' refers to universities, colleges and institutes of higher education.

Acknowledgements

I would like to thank the staff at the University and Colleges Admissions System (UCAS) who have so willingly given help about many things, in particular Mike Scott, University and Colleges Liaison Officer at UCAS, for his comments and advice. Also Erica Fryd at the British Council in London for her patient answers to the many questions; Heist for their help with research documentation; and Dr Allan Johnson at the University of Sheffield who is also President of that wonderfully enthusiastic group of people from the Higher Education Liaison Officers Association (HELOA).

Thanks must also go to Philip Mudd at Kogan Page for his endless support and advice, plus David Greenwood whose interest has been a great encouragement.

Thank you to family and friends for their never ceasing interest. And last but certainly not least, to my partner Paul for his continuing patience, good humour and wonderful support.

O N E

Your future, your choice

The next stage... if you want it

Higher education. It will change you, your life and your bank balance. It will make you richer in experience, knowledge and skills. You'll leave university with a qualification, a completely new circle of friends and contacts and a new way of thinking and looking at things. The words 'why? or 'what if?' will continually spring to mind. You can think for yourself.

You'll spend many nights putting the world to rights over several bottles of cheap wine with your new friends; pull all-nighters to get essays or assignments finished; show freshers or sixth form students around campus; compare debts, rents, and who spends the least every week on heating. You'll ask your parents for more money – just when you thought you had become an independent adult. You'll wander from lecture to coffee bar in the Union and lunch in the Union. It's up to you whether or not you attend your lectures. No one is going to hassle you or keep reminding you that your essay is due Friday week. Never again will your life offer you such freedom in terms of deciding what to do with your day – despite your worries over money and distant thoughts about getting a job. You can do what you like in the holidays – get work experience, travel, work abroad, voluntary work, do nothing, or get a paid job. People at work look back to their university days and remember the freedom it allowed them.

> 'It's a time in your life when you've absolutely no responsibility at all, just the freedom to do as you want. Yes, you'll end up in debt – probably – but you'll have lots of fun, makes loads of new friends and learn a lot about yourself. '
>
> Lucy, modern languages graduate, investment banker

‘You'll never have a better chance to try out new things, meet new people, learn about yourself and study stuff because you're just genuinely interested in it. You just play hard and work hard – the more you put in, the more you'll get out of your university days.’

Amanda, chemistry graduate, secondary school teacher

You might take up a new sport – parachuting, gliding, windsurfing or mountain climbing. You might meet your future partner or employer at university; you may even set up your own business. You'll leave with the confidence that you can handle anything life throws at you and cope with any situation. A university education will expand your horizons – where else can you meet people from such a wide variety of backgrounds – and equip you to cope with change and the unexpected.

Education is an investment – a university degree is no different. You'll invest two, three or four years of your time and money. You'll doubtless end up in debt with loans to pay back and overdrafts to sort out. Students at university today have more worries about money and the job market than their predecessors and many would say that they are under far more pressure. But take heart. Graduate salaries are rising, employers want to recruit employees with strong communication and people skills who can handle changing circumstances, customers and colleagues. They want innovators, managers, people who will develop others and always look for the better way to do something. And if you're a creative person and someone who can network well, the good news is that the market looks particularly encouraging for people who can create their own job and network with others to find out where the opportunities are. The enquiring mind you'll develop at university will serve you well at work.

Thinking about university is a journey in itself, and a very important one. Just when you've probably finished your GCSEs and worked out what you're going to do next (relieved sigh), it's time to think ahead again. Careers staff are muttering strange new words like 'UCAS' and pinning up notices about forthcoming visitors to give talks about higher education courses. Faced with yet more work, pressure from friends and family ('So what are you going to do after A-levels/GNVQ?'), you're also introduced to the huge jungle of higher education. Unfortunately, there's little time to stop the world and get off to have a rest from career planning. Before you know it, your application with up to six choices will need to be in Cheltenham.

It will take loads of energy and enthusiasm and effort to decide what's best for you and apply. The good news is that this journey will equip you with vital skills you'll need throughout your working life, namely decision-making skills. (Many prospective employers will want to know how you came to decide on your university degree and course to see what your career planning skills are like.) Your journey through the career decision-making process may also surprise you, as it suggests opportunities and choices to you that you had not thought possible before.

The important thing is to be able to find the right course for you, which will suit your academic and career interests, meet your values and needs in terms of location and surroundings and give you a happy and successful course. Don't panic. Help is at hand to see you through.

Why look at higher education?

People sign up for higher education courses for all sorts of reasons. Do any of these apply to you?

- To leave home and become independent.
- To have some fun.
- To improve my job prospects.
- To qualify for a career.
- To study or work abroad.
- To prove I can do it.
- To gain skills that will be useful to an employer.
- No idea what else to do – a natural progression from school.
- To combine theory in class with practical work experience.
- To study a subject I enjoy in greater depth.
- To become better acquainted with Britain while studying for a degree.
- To study a new subject.

You can get all these things out of a higher education course. So what's the downside?

- It won't guarantee you a job, but then nothing in life will.
- It won't come cheaply in terms of time or money, but then quality packages never do.
- It won't necessarily move your career thoughts forward unless you make a conscious decision to do some active thinking and planning for the future.

▶ You need to make sure your time at university adds value to your CV – and not just because you can proudly put the word 'degree' on it.

'*Should I be weighing up other options as well as university?*'

Yes, you should. You may find that you don't have to go to university full time to achieve your immediate and long-term goals, because you could achieve them in other ways. For example, in order to meet people and have fun, you could join a volunteer programme or travel, working your way round the world. (But you won't get a qualification at the end of it.) Look at the employment opportunities available locally which involve training programmes for nationally recognised qualifications, such as banking, engineering and hospitality.

Be active in looking around at the alternatives

'Our school only concentrates on higher education; there doesn't seem to be much else around. They never really talk about what else we could do – it's all very vague and frustrating.'

Joanna, lower sixth form student

If you were Joanna, you could:

▶ Ask your careers teacher if representatives from local recruitment agencies can give a talk in school about job opportunities for people who don't want to go on to higher education. If this agency is a national one, so much the better, because they'll be able to give you a national picture as well.
▶ Ask for a representative from the local careers office and Training and Enterprise Councils (TECs) to come in to talk about options after further education.
▶ Spend time in the careers library really checking out the options available in terms of what local employers offer and the opportunities to travel, work, do voluntary work.
▶ Do a job search on the Internet and through recruitment platforms such as JobSite where vacancies are advertised.
▶ Talk to friends, family, friends of the family, anybody you know who may be able to help and put you in touch with people who are recruiting; check local papers, but remember that many vacancies are not advertised.

- ► Talk to the British Council offices if you are an international or EU student and discuss your aspirations with the teachers or tutors at your school or college.
- ► Make use of every opportunity to learn about careers, employment and training. Go to talks and conventions prepared to listen and learn and to move your career thinking forward.

There are usually three conclusions you may reach about any options:

- ► No, that's definitely not for me.
- ► Yes, that looks really interesting, I must find out more.
- ► That looks good, but not quite right – is there anything closely related? (Think laterally.)

Talk about them with your careers adviser.

Tips for making the most of your careers interview
- ► It's your time so make the most of it – turn up, for a start (lots of people don't).
- ► Go with a set agenda of things you want to find out, discuss or need help with.
- ► Come away with an action plan.
- ► Follow up your action plan – or the interview will be a waste of your time.

If your school or college isn't providing what you want in the way of careers education and guidance, don't whinge. Tell the person in charge of careers, and be explicit about the sort of help and information you need. Complaining after you've left won't help you.

'Is higher education for me or not?'

You will need to weigh up taking a full-time university degree course against the other options available to you, taking into account the pros and cons of each option. Choose the one that matches your interests, strengths, values and needs.

In any career plan, there are four parts to making a decision about your future. In this case, these might include the following:

5

1. Knowing yourself
- Your strengths, interests, values, needs, potential, ambition, definition of success.
- How much more immediate training and studying do you want to do? Full or part time?
- What sort of career do you want?
- What difference do you think university courses will make to your job prospects?
- What do you want to get out of higher education?

2. How do you match the opportunities available?
- Now and in the future (ie, what are the growing career areas).
- In your home country and away (ie, internationally).
- In education training and employment on a full-or part-time basis.
- Which of these appeal most?
- How do university courses match up with your needs, interests, and career plans?
- Are they essential to your career plans, helpful, or not necessary?

3. What do you need to do to get there?
- How much more studying do you need to do prior to starting university?
- What qualities will you need to succeed in your application and the course itself?
- How will you finance your preferred option?
- How and when should you apply?

4. How do you make the move?
- Who can you turn to for help and advice?
- Where can you get further information?
- How can you best market yourself?
- What do you need to do to get there? (eg, travel to university, settling in).

To make the decision of whether university is right for you, you'll need a set of decision-making skills. In fact, you'll need these throughout the rest of your life as you change jobs or even careers.

Skills you need (now and throughout your working life)

Communication skills Being able to ask for information clearly in writing and orally

Research skills Knowing how and where to find information; being able to use libraries and information services

Time management Allotting time to research and planning ahead so as not to miss important application deadlines

Analysing information Analysing comments people make about courses and careers so that you can pick out what is useful and what is not

Organising Keeping information together in a file:

(a) about the opportunities available
(b) about you, eg, copies of applications, letters, CVs, forms
(c) clippings from papers about companies, jobs, universities and courses that appeal
(d) advice on what selectors want

Networking Building up a network of contacts who can help you connect with other people

Action planning So that you know what you have to do and how you are going to get there

Asking for help Knowing when you need advice and being able to ask the right people for it

Personal qualities

The ability to be inquisitive Asking questions. What do people do all day at work or at university? What advice do they have?

Persistence Being confident and tenacious

Energy, enthusiasm To get up and make the effort to find things out

Tip: try Centigrade or Course Finder

If you are at school or college, you may have access to Centigrade or Course Finder. These sorts of programmes will match your interests and abilities to courses in higher education. You'll get your own personal report which will point you in the right direction, suggesting courses you might like to start looking at plus a list of universities and colleges which offer suitable courses.

'What sorts of questions should I be asking about the future?'

Get information on the employment market. Make it a five-minute-a-day habit and you'll rapidly build up a picture of employment options, even if you just read the recruitment pages and articles on careers in newspapers. They'll also give hints on what selectors are looking for. Ask questions about the workplace and how university courses may help you in your career plans, such as:

1. Which areas of employment are expanding? Do these interest me and are there university courses to give me the skills, knowledge and recognition from employers I would need?
2. What difference will having fluency in languages make to my future career prospects? What impact will it have on my career if I *don't*? Can I study languages that will give me something different to offer? (And then, do I want to learn a language anyway?)
3. What additional skills can I learn at university that will increase my career prospects, such as competency in information technology, management studies, numeracy?
4. How much responsibility do I want to have? Do I like guiding and leading others? How might university help me develop these abilities?
5. Are there courses that could give me the skills I need to run my own business, to do short-term consultancy work or contract work, either after I have finished or during the holidays?
6. What skills do I enjoy using now? Can I see any of my strengths, likes, interests and passions developing into careers and would a university course cater for these?
7. Do I want work using the specialist knowledge I've acquired at university, applying it to the workplace, or general skills, or a mixture of both? Do I want to study something purely for interest? Which will give me more flexibility in the workplace?

8. Who can I talk to who's knowledgeable about employment? Employers? Personnel officers? Recruitment agencies? Professional organisations? Employees themselves? What sort of qualifications are they looking for? What will they recognise?
9. What do I want to achieve in five years' time? Ten years' time? A professional qualification? Management abilities? My own business? The freedom to travel and work? International experience with a company? Be a director? How might university courses prepare me for my goals?
10. What methods do employers use to recruit people? Will any of these help me while I am at university in paying for my degree course and getting on in work or postgraduate studies afterwards?
11. Do I want to prepare for a career which is likely to be fairly international in flavour?
12. Have I got specific interests I'd like to develop at university that aren't related to the workplace? Will I still be able to get a job afterwards?

Don't expect to be able to answer all these questions now – they are things you should be thinking of as you go, from the start of your journey to research higher education to the day you graduate.

'So, when am I going to have time for all this soul searching and research?'

Manage your time effectively
- Make good use of the holidays. Careers services are open and available even while schools are shut; many people forget this.
- Make good use of public libraries – most have career areas with literature and computer-guided programs.
- Make career planning a priority.
- Keep one day of the week purely for rest and recreation so that you can return to work, school or college fresh in thought.
- Set out your week on a Sunday evening – set targets for all you want to achieve.
- Reward yourself accordingly.

'I have special needs'

If you are a disabled student or if you have learning difficulties such as dyslexia, you may need extra support from the university. If you are in the UK, contact SKILL, National Bureau for Students with Disabilities, for help and advice – their address is in the back of this book. If you are outside the UK, the local British Council will be able to help or you could access it via the Internet. Check out Chapter 6 for further advice.

'What if I want to do my entire degree abroad?'

Whether you are a British student seeking to study for your degree in, for example, the United States, or an EU national or an overseas student looking to study in Britain, there are key questions to ask yourself as you research the options open to you.

► How will a degree taken in my proposed country be regarded by employers back home?
► How will I fund it?

You may decide that you would be better doing some of the degree in your home country and spending a year in Britain as part of the degree through a recognised exchange or Study Abroad scheme.

If you are looking to study in Britain and are not normally resident there, you have a number of options:

► to do the whole degree programme in Britain;
► to do part of a degree in your home country and then enter a related degree course in Britain perhaps in the second year – many universities will consider your previous studies as credit towards their degree courses if the standard is right; this is known as advanced standing;
► to join an exchange scheme, perhaps organised by international offices or departments;
► to do an exchange programme under the auspices of SOCRATES (EU students only; see the Glossary);
► to join a British university for a short period of time such as a year, as a Junior Year Abroad student, or a semester. (Many students find semesters too short to make the most of them; others find they are just right.)

Discuss these options with members of the British Council in local offices or your International Office/Study Abroad Office if you have already started your degree programme in your home country. They will help you decide on the right course of action.

'Am I too old to study for a degree?'

The good news for mature students (students aged 21 plus) is that no, you're not over the hill. Mature students are welcomed warmly because they are very motivated – and consequently very successful. Even if you were a major failure at school ('I left without any qualifications at all') there are routes offering you second chances. So don't worry: you could find yourself doing part-time or full-time study in no time!

'Who needs universities, anyway?'

Did you know that universities provide services for many customers, including:

- students... full-time, part-time, British, overseas, young, old, professionals;
- employers... with students, training current employees, working on technological developments;
- countries abroad... using the expertise of British research and teaching;
- the government... ensuring the country has the right manpower to compete in a global economy, producing research, providing expertise and advice in every area;
- the community... doing research which will affect us all, providing learning opportunities towards degrees or other qualifications;
- academics... undertaking research for their own purposes or contracted by organisations, agencies or governments to do so;
- the media... seeking comments from experts on news items, such as 'What will these terrorists be like?' or 'How far could the recent history of the country impact on developments in...?'

What you have to do is to identify what they can offer you!

SUMMARY EXERCISES

▶ What do universities do? Visit an institution near to you and pick up a prospectus; have a look round to get an initial idea of what a university is like.

▶ Talk to people who have been to university (whatever their age) – what did they do, how did it help their career and what advice do they have?

▶ Why are you interested in going to university? Compare notes with friends who are also interested to see if your reasons are similar. If it's because you don't know what else to do, then:
 – spend time in the careers library researching options;
 – ask your careers teacher to deliver a session on options other than university.

▶ Start identifying your career plans and what you are looking to do in the next five to eight years or so: how will a university education contribute to them?

▶ When you are thinking about future options, ask yourself:
 – how would this option meet my interests, career aspirations and needs?
 – how much will it add to my CV, skills and life experience?
 – how much does this option relate to the job market; will it increase my chances of getting a job later/now? Will it close any doors?
 – what difference will it make later on, eg, to my job prospects? Does it appeal?

Always know how you're future immediate plans may contribute to long-term ones (or at least, how they are contributing to your CV), so that they are never wasted.

TWO

Making use of information and time

Counting down to 15 December, the year before you plan to start university

Assuming that you've passed your GCSEs and that you're in the first year of further education, let's take a look at what you need to do and when you need to do it.

First year in further education

By this time you should have an idea of what your strengths, weaknesses, needs and values are. You should also know what you could do with your post-16 choices and what you can't do. Most further education courses leading to higher education will last two years. After working hard for GCSEs and investigating your further education choices, you may find yourself thinking, 'Great, a breather from thinking about careers.' Sadly, that's not the case. You have to get thinking and planning.

Getting information – where to find it

There is an enormous amount of information available to you on higher education.

'There's far too much information, and too many choices – it makes it impossible to decide what to study, never mind where you're going to study it.'
Breda, lower sixth form student, A-levels in maths, French and biology

However, take heart: there's also lots of help around; heed the advice from this ex-student:

'I did absolutely no career planning when I applied to university, which is something I regret, although I loved every minute of my history degree. I studied it because I was interested in the subject and I was desperate to get out of a secretarial job in a bank. I've always had a passion for history: even now, I walk to the history section of any library I'm in before I check out anything else. However, I must admit that I often look back and wonder how different my life would have been if I'd done some thorough soul searching with regards to my future. (The day I graduated, I still didn't know what I was going to do.) So make use of the information available to you – you never know what you will find.'   The author!

Managing your time and making your decision: a suggested timetable

Autumn
- Get familiar with the resources available to you such as the library, computers, careers staff and the careers service, especially if you've started a new school or college.
- If you're linked to the Internet at school, college or at home, surf the net to check out access it offers to careers information.
- Are you aware of the opportunities coming up to find out about careers such as conventions, talks, etc? Note their dates and make a commitment to go.
- Start to get a knowledge of the range of courses available in higher education to make sure you have a fair idea of what you could do.

Throughout the winter/early spring
- Identify what you want from your higher education course ie, what you want to study.
- Check ECCTIS (computer) and *The University and College Entrance: the Official Guide* to find out which institutions offer the subjects you want.
- Talk to your subject teachers and tutors about the grades you are likely to get – they will be detailing your predicted grades on your UCAS reference in the autumn (six months away).
- Work out strategies for improving your grades and areas of weakness which could affect your choice.

Spring/summer

- List the institutions that offer the subjects you want.
- Identify those whose entry requirements you could match (check *The University and College Entrance: the Official Guide* for an initial indication but then refer to prospectuses).
- Check prospectuses for value-added parts to the degree (eg, computer literacy, numeracy, skills employers want).
- Write for information more specifically – or e-mail – on course content, options available, research interests of staff.

Summer

- Visit a short-list of universities to compare them (optional but particularly recommended if you have disabilities or learning difficulties).
- Ask for alternative prospectuses to get the students' point of view.

Summer holidays

- Practise completing your UCAS form, especially the further information section!
- Use your local careers service, especially if you are unsure about what you are planning or doing.
- Talk to local returning students to find out what they think – see their photographs, ask about facilities, ask if they can put you in touch with people on the course you are interested in.

Second year in further education

Autumn

- Establish your short-list of institutions (up to six) – make sure you would be happy to go to any one of them, because you cannot change your mind after applying.
- Complete your UCAS form and hand it to the person doing the reference – give him or her plenty of time to do this.
- Make sure that you're familiar with the application procedure – and follow it.

Here are the all-important deadlines for application:

October 15   Deadline for applications to Oxford or Cambridge
December 15   Deadline for UCAS

If you are an art and design student, check out your deadlines on pages 106–7.

Your form must be in *at UCAS* in *Cheltenham* by these dates and *not* in the post-box in your home town.

Don't blame subject teachers if your UCAS form is late getting to UCAS because you only gave them the form to complete the reference in early December. They are very busy. *Think ahead.*

'But I haven't got the required qualifications yet. How can I apply?'

Many people get confused by the idea that they should apply for a course while they are still working towards the qualifications required to even start a higher education degree or diploma. The important thing is that you must have met the entry requirements asked of you by the *start* of your degree or diploma course.

If you are an international student, you may find that you need to do a short course in English first, before you do a degree in Britain. Visit your nearest British Council office or talk to your advisers at school or college.

Remind yourself of your network – get help from people you know:

- ► people you know at university or those who have just graduated, eg, past students from school and college – they know what it is *really* like;
- ► people you know who are at work, eg, parents, friends, friends of the family;
- ► employers: people you've done work experience with, paid holiday jobs, part- or full-time work;
- ► people in full-time education eg, careers teachers, head teacher, subject teachers, course tutor, administrators.

They can be useful in giving you lots of useful first-hand information and tips or putting you in touch with people they know in their own network. Be inquisitive: don't be afraid to ask. Most people love to talk about their experiences and if you show them that you are interested and serious about your future, they are likely to be only too happy to help. You will probably be inundated with helpful comments and find that your problem is trying to get people to stop talking!

'University days are the best days of your life!'

> 'Liverpool is a great place to be a student… I wouldn't be anywhere else on earth.' Simon, engineering student, University of Liverpool

When you're getting advice from your contacts, remember that what one person sought from an experience won't necessarily match your own aims and objectives. Some people are much quieter in their enthusiasm than others but equally pleased with their lot. Also bear in mind that the people you talk to may be very out of date – even the application system has changed in the past year – so get the nitty gritty from careers advisers on anything specific. And finally, write to thank those who help you – you may need their help again.

Other ways to make use of contacts:

- shadow a student at a local university or college to get an insight into student life – if they're on the course you're interested in, so much the better;
- sit in on first-year lectures in your proposed subject(s) for a day – ask the lecturer first;
- chat to other students taking the course you want to do.

Your careers teacher may be able to help you arrange these fact-finding missions.

If you are at school or college in Britain already as an international student, ask if you can make a visit to the local university to meet the staff in the International Office; they may have lots of useful tips to offer.

Useful starting points

Talks on higher education

If you are in school or college, a frequent starting point to higher education is 'The Talk', given by a careers officer, a careers teacher or tutor or even a representative from a British university. These introductory sessions cover topics like: what is higher education? What does a university do? What can you study at a university and what should you think about when choosing your course?

Other sessions may be more specific:

> Thursday lunchtime, Careers Room at 1:20
> University Courses in Podiatry.
> All welcome – bring your lunch with you

or:

'Now, next week, we've got a representative from Oxford Brookes University coming to talk about modular degrees, so please ask lots of questions.'   Careers teacher, talking to lower sixth form

Talks such as these *can* be very useful (depending on the speaker). The talk on podiatry (feet and lower limbs) is likely to expand to talk about the range of medically related courses available. Even if you thought you had set your heart on physiotherapy, you may be surprised and realise there's more to feet than meets the eye, so check them out – you may decide that it's podiatry you really want to do.

The talk by the Oxford Brookes representative may open your eyes to a wonderful way to combine subjects if you're not sure about what you want to do, and how modular degrees may be particularly helpful if you don't like taking exams at the end of your course. You'll inevitably find out something about Oxford Brookes University too.

Finally, the speaker is likely to know something of his subject and how it is taught at other universities, because he's working with academics all the time. So think broadly: information is power. At the very least, you can say, 'That's not for me.'

You may also be able to attend a typical first-year lecture delivered by a visiting professor to your school or college, to get an idea of what it would be like to study the subject at university. For example, university staff in robotics engineering may give students doing maths or physics A-levels or GNVQ engineering an introductory lecture into robotics as a taster.

Getting to grips with the range of courses

Careers conventions

In Britain, these will probably be organised by UCAS Education Conventions. They can be very large events, with well over 130 exhibitors in major city venues, or much smaller. Go if you can – you'll have a great opportunity to:

► find out what institutions (and employers) have to offer;
► meet people from those institutions and get answers to questions;
► compare what each exhibitor has to offer that matches your own
  personal interests, career aspirations and potential.

The more preparation you have done before you go to a convention, the more you will get out of it. If you can, you should have a rough idea of what subjects interest you and who will be there that offers them. Try to prepare some questions in advance and come away with information and an action plan so that you use the event as an opportunity to move your career thinking forward.

> ' Don't wander round aimlessly in a group – it's a waste of time, and you'll probably all want to do different things anyway. Go round with a friend or on your own – you'll have a better chance of finding out what you want. '   Leo, GNVQ Business Studies student

Take a copy of your CV with you for ease of reference, as it's always easy to forget vital points when you're suddenly asked questions like, 'Have you got a GCSE Grade C in a science subject?'

Many of the stands will be manned by representatives from the universities and colleges whose job it is to travel around Britain talking to students like you about opportunities in higher education. They are part of a group known as HELOA, which itself is guided by a code of practice and ethics. They are impartial and want to help you. They all know a lot about each other's institutions, because they spend a lot of time at the same events together, so make the most of their knowledge. Although they represent their institution, at the end of the day their main goal is to help you make informed decisions. If they feel their institution is not going to offer what you want, they will point you to one that will. They are a friendly, enthusiastic group of people with boundless energy and many of them are also ex-students so make use of their knowledge and desire to help you.

Many careers conventions will have talks as well: these cover a range of subjects, from 'Choosing your degree course' and 'Filling in your UCAS form' to more specialised subjects perhaps pertaining to popular careers, such as 'What law courses want in applicants' or 'Mathematics courses: an overview'. Some speakers will invariably be better than others (inspiring or yawning delivery), but it's the luck of the draw. Go, listen and reflect how the session has moved your career planning forward.

Conventions are also organised in other countries throughout the world, usually by the British Council offices. They may run either annually or every two years. Representatives attending these events may make a tour of your country afterwards, so check with your local British Council office for dates and times of visits. There may be visiting speakers from British universities that you could meet on an individual basis. They are, after all, coming to meet people like you! Local secondary schools, colleges and universities may also have British academics or visitors coming out to your country so contact them to find out. They may interview you right there and then!

Some British universities have offices abroad to help you; Nottingham Trent University for example has one in Kuala Lumpur. Again, your local British Council can help you identify the network and links British universities have in your region.

Books

The University and College Entrance: the Official Guide (published annually) contains university profiles and lists what you can study where. Start with the 'How to get the best out of this Guide' section. If in doubt, get advice. The index will guide you to the subjects you're interested in. Now start narrowing down your choices by getting a feel for the courses on offer and then work out how closely they match your needs, potential grades and preferences, eg, location in Britain, size. *The Guide* can only indicate the likely requirements that you'll be asked for – you'll need to look at individual prospectuses for more accurate information.

The Guide is available in your careers library at school, but it is often in demand. Try your local public library's reference section as well or visit your local careers service. Alternatively, if you want a copy at home, you could buy one from a bookshop.

The *CRAC Degree Course Guides* are helpful, especially if you've decided on your subject or at least the subject area. You can read around your subject and delve into the sorts of courses on offer within it; it will broaden your thinking. The Guides also give you details of graduate destinations and raise your awareness of what students *do* after a philosophy degree.

If you're doing a GNVQ, check the booklet *GNVQs and Higher Education 1997* produced by the GATE project, which has done loads of research into progression possibilities from GNVQs on to higher education courses. ECCTIS will also be able to provide you with lots of valuable information, including advice for applying to courses. Many institutions have a GATE contact who can give you more information. Careers advisers and careers advisory services will have access to these booklets.

What Do Graduates Do? is a useful annual publication which gives you an excellent insight into what sorts of work graduates are doing.

In addition, a number of guides give more detailed information on each of the universities; they are available from bookshops and careers libraries and their titles are included in the 'Further information' section (p.165).

Information Technology

ECCTIS

ECCTIS is a computerised information service, offering details of nearly 100,000 courses. It works very closely with the information in the *UCAS Handbook*. When you access ECCTIS through the online and CD-ROM services, you will be asked a series of questions to identify the type of course you are looking for in terms of subject, method of study (eg, full- or part-time), institution type and location. ECCTIS displays the details of all the courses which meet your needs and you can also access further information on the course itself, eg, structure, content and length. It also provides admissions details, including information from the GATE database (GNVQ and Access to Higher Education), worth a look at for anyone doing a GNVQ. It will gives mature students information on the opportunities available through Access courses and credit transfer. ECCTIS also gives information from professional bodies and qualifications. ECCTIS is available in public libraries, careers offices, colleges of further education and Training Access Points, British Council offices and many secondary schools in Britain and world-wide. It's fast, you get the information you need within minutes on a computer printout and, especially if you want to combine subjects, you'll find it very easy to use – a lifesaver, in fact.

The Internet

Many universities now have World Wide Web (WWW) sites, giving you access to information about courses and institutions on the Internet. You can therefore find out about universities without leaving your home. Many universities and colleges now have their own web site so you can contact them if you have queries about admissions. For example, the University of Sheffield is on: http://www.Sheffield. ac.uk/uni/admin/admit.

The British Council has a WWW site, giving a vast amount of information and help. You'll find information on English language requirements, how to choose the right institution, the courses available, costs, distance learning opportunities, immigration procedures... it's full of useful details. The virtual campus guide includes institutional profiles of some 200 schools, colleges and universities. It will also give you access to alumni information, and researching and teaching assessments. Log in at: http://www.britcoun.org/eis/ Happy surfing!

Starting to look for more detailed information

Prospectuses

Every university or college has a *free* prospectus with:

► information about the range of courses, course content, entry qualifications, career prospects, opportunities to mix subjects and include work experience or study abroad, learning and assessment methods;
► information on the university itself, its mission or goals, facilities, support systems, student life, location, etc.

You can get a copy of the prospectus by calling the institution or going to the careers library – if it hasn't gone missing already. Many prospectuses have sections for those students who need special support. Universities may also provide brochures specifically for:

► mature students
► international students
► part-time courses
► parents.

Just ask!

Finding out about the course itself

To choose the right course, you need more information than the prospectus provides, so contact the relevant department for:

► a list of current optional courses, reading lists, syllabuses

- data on the members of faculty to see if their research interests match yours; course options are likely to match staff research interests to some extent
- departmental brochures
- details on assessment methods.

You'll get a clearer picture of what the course will be like and whether it will suit you.

Alternative prospectuses

Get a copy from the institution if available. They're written by students and usually well worth a read because they give a vivid description of what it's *really* like to be a student at the University of X.

Open days

Many universities and colleges run open days or visit days to give you the chance to find out first-hand what the institution is like. Visits are always very worthwhile because you'll be able to get a 'feel' for the place and how comfortable you are there. The prospectus is designed to paint a rosy picture – they want you – so the photographs will probably have been taken on a sunny day when everything looks good. Get dates of a few open days for your preferred institutions from your careers teacher, careers service, by calling the institution direct or checking the prospectus. If you can't make the date, see if you can schedule your own visit to meet a representative from the department and current students; most Student Unions will find someone to give you the guided tour so that you can really get a feel for the place and get your many questions answered.

Useful thoughts
- If you need to stay overnight, the School and College Liaison Office should be able to suggest somewhere cheap to stay, but if your school or college has a past student there, why not see if you can sleep on their floor?
- Line up a short-list of universities to visit and compare.
- Don't expect institutions to be able to schedule visits with 24 hours' notice – give them two or three weeks' notice.
- If you're going to invest time and money in a degree course, you should know what you're letting yourself in for.

A typical open day may run something like this:

	University of Hope	
	Content	Contact
Morning	Welcome and introduction Guided tour of the campus and facilities including: • examples of accommodation • library facilities • computing facilities • labs (if appropriate) • Student Union amenities	School/College Liaison Unit Current students
	Lunch	Current students, School and College Liaison staff
Afternoon	Talk by departmental staff • what they look for in an applicant • structure of the course • options available	Academic staff and students
	Interviews (formal or informal, depending on department)	Academic staff
	Guided tour of the town/city (optional)	School and College Liaison staff and students

At the visit/open day

Work out what you want to find out before you go, and you'll get far more out of your visit. In particular, it's worth talking to people on the course you want to do; if this is a daunting prospect, take a list of questions with you – nobody will mind and as you start to question people about the course and life at university, you will probably find that you start talking naturally without worrying about gaps in the conversation. Ask students what their advice would be to you and what they wish they had known before starting a course.

Students themselves can give you an insight into the typical life of a student at a British university. They can tell you all sorts of things, such as how helpful the university staff are, what the resources are like and how much pressure there is to use the computer facilities, books in the library, etc. They will also be able to give you an idea as to the price of a pint, a meal out as a treat, a helping of fish and chips, books, weekly rent, and phone calls home. They will be able to tell you how easy it was to get a place in halls, which landlords to avoid, which are the best pubs and why, what it was like adapting to life in halls, how little money they manage on a week and how much their debt is. (Believe it.) Plus you'll get useful inside information as to the best tutors, who makes you sit up and take interest and who sends you to sleep, how easy it is to get help if you're stuck, what the library is like, what the lecture halls are like, how much work there is to do, what the teaching and assessment methods are like, what activities there are… If you meet graduates who are already at work, try to find out how they thought university life prepared them for the workplace. Remember that departments differ: for example, their resources, teaching styles, accommodation and assessment methods may be completely different, even in one institution.

Parents going to open days

As increasing numbers of parents are attending open days and visits, so more institutions are operating a programme specifically for parents. It is important that parents give sons or daughters plenty of space to look around the campus and ask their questions; parents will have plenty of time to ask separately. If you are going to an open day with your son or daughter, don't bombard them with questions the minute you leave: they will need time to sort their thinking out first; thoughts and comments will flow if you let them. Your interests won't necessarily match theirs; the important thing is that your offspring will be happy and successful.

Obviously, things have changed since your day. If you're seeking information, UCAS produces *The Parents Guide to Higher Education* and you can also get help from your offspring's school or college and seek information from the local Careers Service. Many schools and colleges will also run parents evenings with a talk on higher education, and you will always be welcome at careers conventions and events.

Parents going in to the interview

Some departments allow it, some don't. If you go in to an interview with your son or daughter, remember it's *their* interview. Let them do the talking. You may be paying for some of your 'child's' university career and want to ensure that your questions are answered; but if your son or daughter does not find out the answers he or she needs to make an informed decision, he or she could make a very expensive mistake.

Making the decision: Getting help at home

Careers officers

Careers officers will give you the chance to weigh up all the opportunities, looking at the advantages and disadvantages of each one. They can advise on the application process, suggest options you hadn't thought of and act as a facilitator, for example if you need extra help and support. They will advise you on the sources of information available, suggest events for you to attend and help you put an action plan together. Careers services or advisory companies should have a well stocked, up-to-date library and many offer computer-aided guidance programs and computer-based information, not just about courses but also on jobs. Make use of your local careers service – that's what it's there for. It's free and open throughout the year (including school holidays).

'Who helps mature students?'

Adults should contact careers services listed in the telephone directory. Some give adults careers guidance (you may have to pay); or you could contact your local institution of higher education and see if they have an office which specialises in advising mature students. It may also be worth giving your local Training and Enterprise Council (TEC) a call.

Remember:

- Don't expect your entire career to be laid out within a half hour's interview. It may take several visits to the careers teacher before you have even decided what course you want to do.
- If you don't get anything out of your careers interview, you could

26

do two things: ask for another one – it could have just been an off day for the careers adviser or you; or see another counsellor for a fresh point of view.

Your subject teachers and tutors

- ► Beware: they may be out of date with the higher education scene.
- ► They may try to push you towards studying 'their' subject at their favoured institutions.
- ► They may be able to link you with particular contacts they have.
- ► They can help you assess your strengths and interests, and look at your future potential.
- ► Take their comments and advice as a part of the whole picture of information – at the end of the day, it's your decision.

The press

The press can be both a negative and positive force in the search for the right course. Newspapers frequently include articles which may be useful in terms of:

- ► identifying employment trends and job growth areas
- ► giving advice about applying for courses or jobs – ie, what selectors look for
- ► showing vacancies for courses or paid employment, full- or part-time
- ► information and advice about Clearing
- ► highlighting employers and institutions you could apply to.

The press may also spread unnecessary negative thinking and panic. Human nature being what it is, bad news sells – so try not to panic in August when you see headlines like, 'No places in Clearing' or 'Standards now lower than 20 years ago'. Concentrate on yourself. Press headlines will still be going on about issues such as these long after you've gone and graduated.

Television

Programmes may help to increase your information base about jobs and careers. During Clearing, there's advice on television and radio about what to do. Television may provide insights into careers, and even broaden your horizons in terms of the careers available; many presenters are past graduates, not in journalism studies, but in things like chemistry or maths. Remember that your weekly viewing of 'Animal Hospital' alone won't convince veterinary admissions tutors that you have thoroughly researched being a vet and thereby decided it's positively for you. In fact, it's probably better not to mention it at all.

Your careers teacher in school or college may also show you a series of six television programmes made for the BBC called 'A Life of Knowledge'. Pay attention – don't doze off in the corner or wonder what you're going to wear for that all-important date!

Videos

Many institutions produce videos to give you a good idea of what their campus is like; this is particularly useful if you are abroad and hoping to study in the UK. These videos may give a good indication of the campus and surrounding scenery and they usually make the place look good, so try to look at returning students' photographs as well or visit.

UCAS

UCAS is a body containing considerable expertise on higher education in Britain. It will process your application and give advice about the application procedure. It plays no part whatsoever in the selection process. More on UCAS in Chapter 7.

Getting sponsorship

Many people are sponsored through higher education by an employer or organisation. This means they may have their tuition fees paid for them, plus they may receive a salary or living allowance. Pros to sponsorship include:

- you may be guaranteed a job after you graduate
- you're less likely to end up in debt
- you get really useful work experience
- you get insight into the workplace
- you can put theory into practice at once.

Before you enter into a sponsorship agreement, ask these questions:

- Does it last for the entire course?
- Are you restricted to studying at certain universities the employer has links with?
- Will you have to take specific options on the course to meet the employer's needs?
- What happens if you suffer a bereavement or illness during the course?
- What are your obligations in the holidays and after the degree?
- What happens if you fail?
- What does the sponsorship cover?
- What happens if the company goes bust or is involved in a takeover or merger?
- What happens if you want to change sponsors, courses or universities?

Some employers expect you to remain with them for a period of time after completing your degree; others do not. Not all sponsorship necessarily leads to firm employment after you've finished.

The *Which Guide to Sponsorship* will help you identify possible sponsors and the Careers and Occupational Information Centre also provide a booklet, *Sponsorships*, which lists those available from employers and professional bodies. Research your options early on.

Professional organisations

Professional organisations are a mine of information about their own career areas. They set the standards of conduct and activity so as to protect the public from cowboys. Professional bodies and organisations also set the guidelines for training and qualifications. Some have an education or careers sections specifically for people seeking advice. They can guide and advise you about professional qualifications and send you list of accredited degree programmes so that you can gain exemption from professional exams if you study at certain institutions. Get the addresses from *Occupations*, available in any careers library.

Get nosy and research careers. Yours.

There's masses of information available on graduate careers, produced in booklet form. Details of these booklets can be obtained from CSU Ltd (see 'Further information' p.165).

Help at the university

Getting through to universities and colleges

You can reach institutions of higher education through:

- telephone
- fax
- mail
- the Internet
- writing a letter to the right department or the External Relations department.

The University and College Entrance: the Official Guide and *UCAS Handbook* will have many of these addresses.

Admissions tutor

Most departments or courses have an admissions tutor who makes the decision about whether or not you are accepted on to the course. He or she, or the departmental secretary, will be able to give you specific details about entry requirements.

International students should talk about their qualifications with the international office or a representative at the British Council office closest to them, or careers staff in their school.

Marketing department

The marketing department may consist of marketing professionals, plus school and college liaison officers who travel around the country promoting their institution, external relations officers, public relations staff, the international office, European Liaison unit, etc. The composition of the department will vary from one university to another.

Some universities have a 'shop' right in town where you can get help and advice from a team of counsellors who will help you find the right course for you. This can be particularly useful for mature students, whose entry requirements are not always as rigid as would first appear. The University of Wolverhampton for example has a 'Higher education shop' offering prospective students advice and information.

University Careers Service

This should have details about where past students have gone after completing their course. Have a good look at the service if you can while visiting. Is it well stocked? Is it easy to find your way around? Are there lots of people using it? Are the staff friendly and approachable? Are there lots of events going on, eg, talks, visits, employers coming to interview? What do the students on campus think of it? Most services also keep destination statistics enabling you to see where past students have gone after finishing their courses. This is useful information, although employment markets and methods of finding work are changing quickly.

Accommodation office

This is responsible for all accommodation throughout the university. Many institutions give priority to overseas students when allocating spaces in the halls of residence, but they do make an effort to house all first-year students. Alternatively, accommodation offices will provide lists of suitable housing in the area and help you find somewhere to live.

Student Union

The Student Union has its own building, which usually houses services like the welfare office, counselling service and health service. The Union can offer advice and help throughout your course. They'll also find someone who can show you around. The Union represents students' interests on various committees throughout the university or college.

Special Needs Office

This office will help if you have particular requirements, such as a disability or learning difficulties. Make contact with them early on to get the help and advice you need.

International Office

The international office at every university helps and advises students all over the world who want to study in Britain. They will advise on the range of courses available to you and help you decide which level is best for you, whether you want to study for the whole degree in Britain or just a short period of time. They should be able to advise on pre-arrival and induction information, immigration issues, extending and renewing visas, travel information and credit transfer. They will send out information written for overseas students, be able to answer any queries you have and may take charge of liaising with the accommodation office for you.

Going back to full time education after a long break?

Your first port of call should be to the mature students' office if there is one, or the Access and Continuing Education Centre. These can be reached via the main switchboard at your local university. You could also talk to the admissions tutor of the course you want to do about your background and current qualifications to decide a suitable way forward.

Tip: spend some time in the university careers library to see if they have any information about the destinations of mature students. It may help you choose the right sort of course.

Which level of course is for you?

Universities and colleges offer different levels of entry, from foundation or year 0 courses and higher national diplomas to diplomas of higher education, degrees and then postgraduate courses. The level of course that's right for you will depend on:

- your qualifications to date
- whether you are already at work, seeking to gain further qualifications
- whether you need further qualifications before starting a degree.

To ascertain the level which is right for you:

- check the entry requirements for the courses which interest you
- talk to an adviser if necessary (especially helpful for mature students and international students)
- if you are at work, talk to your supervisor or human resource department: your employer may be prepared to sponsor you through a relevant part-time degree.

If you are a Scottish student looking to study in England or Wales, talk to your adviser about whether you should do another year in the sixth form before starting your course. Otherwise you will be a year younger than most people – this can make a tremendous difference, and you may find courses at English and Welsh universities to be very demanding.

Checklist: What do I need to know about the higher education process in Britain?

If you are going to choose the course and place that are right for you, you should know:

► The geography of Britain: regional differences, main cities and towns, the location of universities and colleges (well, roughly).
► What opportunities there are to study in Britain, and have a rough idea of the range of courses and how they meet your interests, strengths, values and needs.
► Application procedures, etc for the whole degree (ie, a British qualification) or part of a degree.
► Where to get more information on these.
► What sort of help each university you're interested in gives students, especially if you are likely to need specialist help.
► The cost and means available of paying for tuition, fees and living costs, and the resources available.

SUMMARY EXERCISES

▶ Take a subject you would like to study at university; if you are unsure, take your favourite of the courses you are following now. Use *The University and College Entrance: the Official Guide* to find out where you can do this subject on its own.

▶ Take the institution which seems to list the most number of courses you could do, involving your favourite subject. Check the number of combinations. Which if any appeal?

▶ Find a copy of the prospectus in the careers library. Look through it and list three points which appeal to you about it and three which don't.

▶ Use ECCTIS to make a print-out of the places offering your favourite subject; e-mail the institution if you can for a copy of a prospectus.

T H R E E

Which course is for you?

When deciding which course is for you, there are some golden rules to follow if you want to choose the right one:

1. Courses with the same title won't necessarily be the same. Psychology at the University of East Anglia could be very different at Portsmouth. One course may suit you better than the other. Geography may be taught as a science or a social science and the entry requirements may differ as a result. Read about your proposed subjects using the *CRAC Degree Course Guides*. Compare course information in a few prospectuses. Decide which angle is best for you.
2. If you're looking for a course with an international flavour, don't sweat. Every course can be studied from this angle – even most medical courses may enable students to have experience abroad. Check the grant implications before you sign up, however.
3. Get as much information as you can on each course from the individual departments concerned and current students. Many students drop out because they chose the wrong course.
4. If you are looking at studying a new subject, make sure you can provide yourself with evidence that it really will hold something for you and make you want to hit those books, the library and the computer.
5. Digest the information available to you carefully – don't skim it and think it doesn't matter. You'll inevitably miss the bit that matters the most.

When you're looking at a specific course, find out:

► Are there any compulsory (known as core) parts?
► How flexible is the course? Can you change your initial preference once you're there?

► How early do you have to specialise? Some places will give you a very general first year (Part One) and then you start focusing on a subject for the next two years (Part Two).

Institutions will differ – check the prospectuses carefully.

Choosing your degree

Initial thoughts to bear in mind

► Forty to fifty per cent of graduate employers don't require a specific degree subject, but many do indicate a preference for those who can show aptitude in numeracy, computer literacy and technology.
► Students taking science, technology and engineering courses will have the widest range of choices afterwards: they can consider careers in which subject choice is irrelevant, plus areas like research and development where their technical skills and knowledge are in demand.
► Students with an element of work experience in their courses tend to find work more quickly than those who do not, and they also feel more confident that they will be able to find a job; they can talk the business lingo!
► Your personal qualities, skills and attitude are as important in getting that job as your degree qualification.
► An early career choice may be right for some people but not for others.

Which course is the right one for *me*?

There's a wide range of courses in higher education for you to choose from. Some subjects may appear to be old hat to you: biology, physics, history, English literature, although even these will be different at university and the subject which was so familiar to you in sixth form or college suddenly takes on a new face. The fact you're listening to a lecture on Albert Camus with what seems like *hundreds* of other students doesn't help. ('There were only 18 in my A-level French group.') Other subjects will be new and exciting: public relations, aeronautical engineering, archaeology. Whatever you study, you must be able to convince yourself – and the admissions tutors – that it is something that makes you feel:

- excited... looking forward to it
- itching... to get your hands on it or you mind to work
- passionate... so that you argue for hours about it
- worthwhile... you're contributing to it
- hungry for more
- challenged
- that you're doing exactly what you want to do, even if you aren't absolutely sure of your ultimate career goal
- that you want to go the extra mile to learn about it or do it.

If it's anything less, ask yourself if it's *really* what you want. You have to be motivated to succeed in higher education in Britain, and if you aren't interested in your subject, your motivation may take a rapid dive.

What are you passionate about?

If you have a long term career goal – midwife, architect, interior designer – it is probably easier to work out which course is for you. Vocational or professional courses have similar course content, because they have to meet specific requirements laid down by the relevant professional body.

If you haven't got a clue, it may be easiest to start thinking about your future course by looking at what really interests you. This could be a favourite subject at school or college which you find yourself naturally working for more than others, because you enjoy it and find it the most interesting. Some people hope that a particular hobby they do at home can develop into a career. What automatically draws your attention, interest, time and energy? How long will this last and how far do you want to remain involved in it? Here are some testers:

- ► Do you learn about it purely of interests sake, ie, out of a formal educational setting, meddling with it at home?
- ► If you won the National Lottery, would you still have an interest in the subject? how much?
- ► Do you read books and trade magazines on the subject outside of class because you want to?
- ► How far do you want to take your interest? As a hobby? As part of a course at university? or enough to make it your life's work?

Here are some factors you could use to look for your degree choice. See if any of them relate to you.

'I want to do the subject I enjoy most of all'

Many people finishing GCSEs will invariably sigh with relief because they think, 'Thank God, no more maths/art/French.' You can study the stuff you really enjoy and find interesting.

At university, you could pick up your favourite academic subject(s):

'I wanted to study maths'	Single honours degree
'I want to study maths and Japanese equally'	Joint honours degree
'I want to study maths most of the time plus Japanese the rest of the time'	Maths is your major, Japanese your minor

Many institutions let you do a 'subsidiary' course designed to further your understanding and knowledge of your main subject. Thus, as a politics student you could study a sociology subsidiary.

You could specialise within your favourite subject:

‘As a history student, I've always enjoyed medieval history the most so I chose a degree which concentrated solely on that.’

> Janice, medieval history student, second year

‘I'm fascinated by immunology, so I'm looking for a degree in it – I may combine it with genetics, I'm not sure yet. My boyfriend Peter is into sea life – he's looking at marine biology. Susie in our group is going to do a mainstream general biological sciences degree, 'cos she doesn't want to specialise yet.’

> Heidi, sixth form student, looking to specialise

Or do something related to it:

‘I enjoyed geography at school – especially the science element – but I'd had enough of it and wanted to do something more relevant to environment. My environmental science course covers lots of geography and science, but it's moving me on to new ground.’

> Karen, first-year student, sought something new

Lots of courses offer you the chance to branch out into new areas:

> ‘I enjoyed doing my sciences, but I wanted to move away and do something which was related to them. My careers teacher suggested I look at food technology or food quality – my course is fantastic, because I'm using my previous knowledge but it's all new. I want to work with a major food manufacturer when I graduate, testing food quality.’   Mark, food science student, enjoying a fresh start

'I'm not sure. Can't I keep my options open?'

Introducing the module
Increasingly, British higher education courses consist of modules or 'units' of study. A unit may last a semester (15 weeks), or one academic year. The unit which lasts a semester means that you can cover more options, but some academics would argue that this leads to more superficial study. They say taking a module over a year means you can probably study it more extensively and in greater depth.

British institutions 'modularised' courses to provide you with more flexibility and choice. You can take modules from different subject areas and, to make international study programmes easier, many international universities work on a modular system of units and credits.

Modular degrees enable you to develop your own course of study – useful if you are not sure what you want to do at university. Some programmes offer more choice than others, so read the prospectus carefully to determine course flexibility: get advice if you're stuck. You are usually assessed module by module – so you don't have to worry about three-hour exams at the end of your three years.

The disadvantages are that you will be expected to be able to plan your own programme with a fair degree of independence. There may be very little support when you come to plan your programme of study at the institution itself. Also, the modules available generally depend on staff research interests (get a list of these from the department) and links with other areas of the university. You should be able to take a subject from another department.

Combined honours degrees usually let you choose courses from a limited number of subjects so they aren't as flexible, but nevertheless they are useful for combining areas of study which appeal to you.

'I want a course which will develop my talent in...'

If you have a talent like writing, acting, music, sport or art, you'll need to decide:

► Are you going to try to make your talent into a career? Are you good enough to become the next Picasso, Lineker, Phil Collins, etc? Get advice from a specialist.
► Are you going to try to use your talent as part of your career, eg, as a dance teacher or art therapist?
► Are you going to keep your talent as a hobby and enjoy it as a break from the real career choice?

'My art teacher said I was good enough to go on to art college, but I decided to do something more business-oriented and keep my art to enjoy as a hobby. It was a hard decision, because I really loved art at school – but now I appreciate it even more. It's very relaxing after a hard week at work to go home at the weekend and paint.'
    Sarah, economics graduate, sales and marketing, tour operator

'Can I take a hobby or interest at home and find a course to develop it?'

Hobbies and interests at home may also indicate possible careers for you. If you are *continually* into these sorts of hobbies, here are some examples of courses you could look at. You could end up running your own business!

Your hobby	Possible courses
cooking	catering management
mending bikes, making models	mechanical engineer
redesigning the inside of your home	interior design, furniture design
gardening, garden design	horticulture
art history	history of art, museum work, gallery
makeup and costume	theatrical design
golf	golf management, leisure studies
horses	equine studies, equine management, leisure studies

40

Check that you fully understand what the course content will involve.

> 'I'm studying for an HND in golf course management. I've always played golf although I'm not good enough to play professionally; I thought it would be great to maintain my interest in the sport through the career. This course is amazing and I'm glad I checked the content out before I signed up – we're doing all sorts of stuff like crop protection, irrigation, plant growth and nutrition and land and soil assessment. Obviously the course and conditions have to be absolutely right for people to play and enjoy the game – but when I first started checking out these courses, I was surprised by the science content. It makes sense now, though.'
>
> James, HND golf course management student,
> looking to manage a Scottish golf course later

'I want to study a subject which is a world-wide concern'

Universities offer courses in international relations, environmental studies, peace studies, war studies, environmental protection and disaster management. Their academics do valuable research and are often called to assist on or comment on relevant situations. If you want to work for a charity or international organisation and apply your new-found knowledge and skills, talk to employers in these areas about the best way in. You should also check what the destinations of past students have been. Any course can have an international perspective. What about geology and international applied geology, for example?

'I want to prepare for an international career'

Increase your job chances by:

- offering at least one other language in a business setting and preferably something that will to make you a bit different: *everybody* does French;
- prove that you can work abroad with people of another country;
- show that you understand how different cultures can affect business;
- understand how information and communications technology can contribute to an organisation's goals.

'I want to develop specific skills I enjoy using now for a specific career'

If you want to train for a specific career, as opposed to doing an arts, social science or humanities course, but you're not sure what, think about the skills you enjoy using – and are good at – and relate them to careers. Look back at your work experience. Is there any particular aspect which appealed to you? Could you see your skills in that area expanding into a career? Examples of how skills relate to careers are as follows:

Your greatest skill or strength	*Possible careers*
promoting causes, products, people, organisations	public relations
solving practical problems	engineering
helping others	social work
developing people	educating, training, management
improving quality	quality management
selling goods	retail management
caring for people who are ill	nursing, radiotherapy
caring for people in an emergency	paramedical science
organising	event management

All of these careers will have specialist areas of their own. For example, if you are looking at engineering, you could check out courses in transport, design, construction (bridges, roads, buildings), power (electrical, electronic, nuclear), resources (mining, water) and land (coastal). Or you could do a general engineering course. If you want to train to be a nurse, you could specialise in adult, mental or children's nursing.

'How do I work out which course I want?'

- ► Read information from relevant professional bodies (check *Occupations*; see 'Further information' p.165).
- ► Talk to local employers.
- ► Ask them for a period of work experience, preferably with a couple of different organisations.
- ► Decide whether you are committed to an area or whether you want a course which gives you general skills and knowledge.

- Look up the right courses on ECCTIS or *The University and College Entrance Guide.*
- Decide if you want a sandwich course, exemptions from professional exams, etc.

'I want a course which will help me go into management'

Many employers take graduates on to management programmes, regardless of their degree discipline. You could therefore study your preferred subject of interest – say geography – and work on developing your transferable skills throughout your course in extra curricular activities (leading a committee, organising an event, presenting material to different groups, working as a team, etc). You could also pick up management options with your degree subject, so that you major in chemistry but pick up units in management studies. Or you could study a general management degree or specialise in areas like:

waste management	leisure management
international management	marketing management
information management	retail management
construction management	operations management.

So there's a wide range to choose from! Fortunately, some areas will appeal to you more than others. Define how large a part of your degree the management part should take up – and you'll start working out whether you want your whole degree in management, whether you want to specialise, or to add on special units.

'I want to add a language'

You don't have to have prior knowledge of a language to study it; somewhere in the UK there should be a course which gives you the chance to learn from scratch. (Some courses want proof that you can handle language learning at an advanced level, but not all of them.) In the competitive world of business, there's a rising belief that you should be able to do business with your clients in their language. So think about it. It's an extra skill to offer an employer.

If you want to study languages, ask yourself:

- Which language(s) do I want to study? You've a wide choice, from Portuguese to Russian, Swahili to Croatian, Korean to Japanese.
- What is my goal in learning a language? Do I want to use it in business? Just be able to speak it for the love of it? Apply it in a technical or scientific context? (The University of Kingston runs a BSc in French for students who want to work in a scientific field in France.) Some courses will offer more vocational language courses (applied languages) than others (German literature).
- Do I want to follow studies relating to a country or a geographical area, such as 'East Asian Studies' or 'Celtic Studies'?

  'I'm studying Russian studies. As part of the course, I do the Russian language, Russian history, geography, politics, society and literature. This means that the course is a very broad one: if I want to concentrate on one aspect more than another, I can. Next year, I'm going to do more Russian politics and geography as those are the areas I want to concentrate on. '

  Peter, Russian studies, second-year student

- Do I want to include a language as an optional unit to study (such as you could do at the University of Greenwich, whatever your course)?

Work out why you want to learn languages and what you hope to do with them. Then you'll be better placed to find the course to suit you.

'I wanted to be a doctor/vet but I know I'm not going to get the grades'

Don't despair. Think broadly and look at the courses offering an interest in medically-related fields or animal science. You could for example check out courses such as:

Animal behaviour	Animal care
Animal management	Animal production
Animal technology	Dairy herd management
Domestic animal science	Equine science
Fisheries science	

The grades required for these courses are likely to be lower, the initial training shorter and, depending on the course, you could still find yourself working with animals (and their owners) in a care capacity.

Tips: Applying for medicine or dentistry?

The Council of Deans of UK Medical Schools and Faculties recommend that you use no more than five choices from the possible six available for either medical or dental courses. You can use the remaining slots for alternative courses without prejudice to your commitment to either medicine or dentistry. Some courses require you to be immunised for Hepatitis B before you start your course. Get your careers teacher to bring a doctor, vet or dentist into school to hear first-hand what the training and job are really like.

Some medical or dental courses:

- ► enable you to take an extra year to study for a BSc
- ► give you units in management science
- ► offer optional units in a foreign language.

'I want to gain skills and knowledge for a specific career with exemptions from professional qualifications'

There is a wide variety of vocational courses at university. Check to see how closely each university links with employers and the relevant professional bodies so that you can ensure they are equipping you with the skills and knowledge employers will need.

Town planning, quantity surveying, medicine, interior design, nursing, physiotherapy, equine management, insurance, graphic design, leisure planning, marketing, engineering, computer science, operations management, financial studies… the list is endless. These courses are not always degree level, nor are they necessarily three or four years long. For example, the University of Central Lancashire runs a University Diploma in newspaper journalism, a one-year full-time course. Higher National Diplomas are a fast way to pick up the relevant skills you need for work so that you can hit the ground running; they are available in vocational, work-related subjects and often lead to exemptions from professional exams.

Tip: get information on the destination statistics of the past students on the courses you're looking at. If most of them went on to further study, that should be a warning that you may need to do a postgraduate course.

'I want to study a course that's vocational but not seriously so in terms of placements and the like'

There are a number of courses which are vocational in that they cover areas like media studies, business studies, leisure studies, travel and tourism studies. They will further your knowledge of these areas, but won't grant you professional exemptions, student membership of societies or, usually, include work experience.

The danger is that you may expect degrees like 'media studies' for example to be highly practical and give you the training you need to contribute to the workplace at once. Some media studies courses are more theoretical and students find they need to do a postgraduate vocational course (thus extra expense) before they find work. Look carefully at graduate destinations for media studies, tourism studies, leisure studies, etc. Check to see how much employer involvement there really is.

'I want to be able to plan a degree to suit my own needs'

You can do this. Independent studies degrees are offered at a number of universities and may be taken up if you have a particular career aim, or want to develop a specific interest of your own. You will probably develop your degree in close cooperation with your tutor; but you spend much time researching, studying and taking courses throughout the university curriculum that are relevant to your subject. Self-motivation is vital. You will also need to be skilled in explaining the course to prospective employers.

Thinking further

Pros of studying academic courses

- You can study a subject you love to greater depth, and aspects of a subject you really enjoy.
- You could study more than one subject as joint honours or in a modular degree.
- You can keep your options open, eg, go on to do more research, a postgraduate vocational course or look for work where your discipline does not matter.

► You could use your knowledge in your future career to work with your hobbies and interests.
► You'll acquire an enquiring mind and intellectual qualities which question everything – qualities employers like.

Cons

► You will need to show employers what transferable skills you've acquired during your degree, so you need to track them carefully.
► You will need to actively seek work experience, paid or unpaid, to gain insight into different careers so that you can contribute more quickly to the workplace.
► You may finish your course not knowing where you want to go next if you don't get exposure to the workplace during your degree.
► Funding could be a problem for vocational postgraduate degrees.

Pros of studying courses with a vocational slant

► If you choose the right course, your degree could lead to professional exemptions and provide a jump start to your career.
► Some careers have only one route via certain degree courses.
► Courses may include work experience which gives you practical skills you can display in the job market.
► May bring you into contact with employers who may contribute to course delivery and development.
► Many students find it easier to get jobs.
► You could study a combination of subjects such as business studies and Japanese.

Cons

► If you change your mind about continuing your career choice after university, you will need to convince future prospective employers of your reason for doing so.
► Many students may worry about choosing a vocational degree in case it restricts their choice.

'I did my degree in architecture, but decided that I didn't want to be an architect, so I had a complete career change. It took me some time to work out what I wanted to do; I took some time out after university and spent a lot of it counselling students locally back home. Eventually, I decided to train as a careers officer, because I enjoyed helping people and seeing practical solutions to problems.'
  John, architecture graduate, careers officer, privatised careers service

At the same time, you need to be realistic. Here are some things to think about:

► What does the course cover? How scientific or technical is it?

'I signed up for a degree in exercise science, because I liked PE at school and I was in a number of teams. Unfortunately, I've had to drop out – I didn't research the course properly and thought exercise science was just going to be sport. I never expected there to be such a high science content. I wish I'd checked out the course content more thoroughly, but to be really honest, I couldn't be bothered – it seemed like too much hassle at the time.'
  Sammi, ex-exercise science student

► Where do graduates go after completing the course?
► Will the qualification travel? How will employers overseas view it?
► Are there any immediate links you can make with local employers who may be able to offer you work experience to help you decide if it's the right sort of career for you?

Investigating a career? Get information first hand. Companies and employers may be able to:

► offer you work experience so that you can check the career is right for you;
► put you in touch with other employers in a different firm, eg, private vs public, small vs large so that you can compare them;
► help broaden your career thinking by giving you experience in different parts of their company;
► sponsor you through the course;
► give you hints as to what they want in a graduate so that you can lay the ground while you are at university.

'What do I need to get in?'

Each course at every institution will apply its own criteria for entry, as well as the institution's general guidelines. The specific course entry requirements will depend on the demand for the course: the more popular courses ask for higher grades. Some subjects – arts, humanities and social sciences – are in greater demand than others like engineering. You may well meet the grades indicated in the prospectus, but that doesn't mean that you'll get an offer. If the competition is strong for a course, many people who are predicted to get the sorts of grades the admissions tutors are looking for may still be rejected because they lack other necessary criteria.

Tip: if you're a Scottish student looking at attending an English or Welsh university, it may be worth spending another year in the sixth form. Otherwise, your fellow students at university will otherwise all be a year older than you are.

Check entry requirements carefully to choose your institutions realistically. Different levels of courses will have different entry requirements. Are you taking these courses?

- General National Vocational Qualifications
- Scottish Higher Certificate
- Irish Leaving Certificate
- International Baccalaureate
- A-levels or AS-levels
- or if you did a BTEC, National Diploma or Certificate.

If so, here's a three-point plan to increase your chances of getting accepted. If you want to hedge your bets, it's up to you, but the successful student will try to minimise the risk of wasting choices by making sure that their initial selection of universities is a realistic one. There is little point in applying for a course which wants three A grades on entry if your teachers are telling you that you are more likely to get two C grades and a D.

1. Start with *The University and College Entrance: the Official Guide*, ECCTIS or *Degree Course Offers* to get an indication of likely entry requirements. Match these roughly in line with your predicted grades – choose some courses which will stretch you to get the results you need and some where you feel you'll comfortably get the grades required. Thus the GNVQ student could look for some

courses demanding distinctions and others seeking merits; you're hedging your bets again in case anything goes wrong.

2. Then turn to the prospectus to get more accurate information on:
   - specific requirements about grades to be acquired
   - specific demands in terms of the subjects or units you should have taken by the start of the course
   - requirements in terms of GCSE grades and subjects
   - other specific details such as interviews, police checks (careers involving children), immunisations required (medical and dental courses).

3. Once you've got a short-list of places which meet your predicted grades, you can start applying personal values and needs, such as 'I want to be in a city' or 'I want to be by the coast'.

Note that you cannot be absolutely certain of what grades you'll need to get until you receive your offer through the post. If you are under 21, you should normally have obtained the minimum qualifications detailed in the prospectuses.

'What can I do to increase my chances?'

You can help yourself by researching the options as early as possible and with care, so that you can plot your further education course accordingly. Make good use of careers conventions, *The University and College Entrance: the Official Guide* and individual prospectuses. If you're still in doubt as to what will be required of you, contact the admissions tutor for the course. Most GNVQ students, for example, should contact the GATE officer at the institutions they are considering applying to.

Some courses require that you study specific units, for example if you're taking a GNVQ, or they may want an A-level. Get your coursework finished well on time – some GNVQ students have failed to get in to university because they were behind with their coursework. Get any relevant work experience you can – it shows evidence of interest and is particularly important if you are applying for a vocational course – and be specific about the transferable study skills you've developed in your further education which will be helpful at university, like research, time management, any presentations you've had to do, planning your own course and choosing units yourself. Above all, be realistic.

'How does the points system for A-levels work?'
Currently, it works in this way:

A-Levels	AS-Levels
A = 10 points	A = 5 points
B = 8 points	B = 4 points
C = 6 points	C = 3 points
D = 4 points	D = 2 points
E = 2 points	E = 1 point

A typical offer could ask for 22 points, without any further details, ie, they don't necessarily mind how these 22 points are made up, so you could get:

History	B	(8)	*or*	History	A	(10)
French	B	(8)		French	C	(6)
English	C	(6)		English	C	(6)
Total:		22 points		Total:		22 points

Note that *The Guide* and ECCTIS can only provide you with an indication, not a firm grade requirement.

Tip: admissions tutors look at your GCSE results for an indication that you have the ability to succeed. If you have not got a C grade in English and mathematics, you could see if your further education courses cover mathematics and English at a level equivalent to GCSE; if it does, ask your referee to point this out as fully as possible – or retake them at night school

International qualifications

How is your English?

Overseas applicants coming to UK universities must show their prospective university that they will be able to cope with following courses in English at degree level. Prospectuses list the standards they expect and the tests they will accept. Many of these are held early in the year, so you should check dates with your local British Council office.

You may need to study English for up to a year before your course starts – many universities run English for Academic Purposes courses, or you may be advised to do an international foundation course to prepare you for higher education, either at the same institution or at another. Successful completion does not guarantee you entry to higher education courses.

You can obtain advice and information on the suitability of your current qualifications for entry to university and whether your English is sufficiently fluent from:

- International offices at the universities themselves.
- British university representatives coming out to visit.
- Your local British Council office.

An organisation called NARIC (National Association Recognition Information Centre) can give you a certificate outlining what the equivalencies of international qualifications are. Their address is in 'Further Information'. There may be a fee.

Mature students

You're in a different position to the student under 21. Admissions tutors will seek evidence of recent serious academic study relevant to the degree as proof of your interest and that your study skills are up to date.

Your three-point plan to get in is to:

1. Get in touch with the admissions tutor for the course or any specific office at the university which specialises in advising mature students.
2. Discuss your background with them, giving them details of your work experience and educational history.
3. They will help you devise an action plan for getting your study skills up to date and picking up the knowledge you need (if any) for your proposed course.

Some options they may suggest you follow are:

- Access or Pathways course – one year, usually taught at a college of further education to prepare you for a degree; a fast-track route!
- Taking a module in the year prior to starting the degree to prove that you can do it.

- Doing a relevant A-level at evening class.
- Picking up a study skills course or making use of the learning support unit if there is one.

Many institutions will take your previous learning and work experience into account. Any professional exams you've done, where relevant, may be accredited to your degree programme, which may reduce the work you need to do to graduate. This may also apply if you've worked for relevant National Vocational Qualifications.

'What about my Higher National Diploma/Certificate?'

If you've studied for an HNC while you're at work, and you want to continue on in a relevant degree subject, you may be able to start into the second year of a degree programme. Contact the Admissions Tutor and see if you can negotiate your way on; if there's no close correlation between your HNC or HND and the degree, you may need to start from scratch.

'What about O-levels? Are they still accepted?'

O-levels are still accepted and known to admissions tutors; if a course demands a specific GCSE subject in a grade and you have an O-level or CSE, check with the relevant admissions tutor that this is sufficient; it should be.

'Help! I want to do aeronautical engineering, but I've done the wrong further education course!'

Courses involving science, technology and engineering are more stringent about sticking to entry requirements than those in the arts and humanities. Take heart. Try a foundation course or an extended degree. These last a year and are usually designed to prepare people who have insufficient or inappropriate academic qualifications for degrees in sciences, engineering and technology. Successful completion enables you to continue on to the degree in a relevant subject. Students on an extended degree are eligible for a mandatory local educational authority grant for the full length of the extended course. If the foundation year forms an integral part of a course attracting a mandatory award, your grant should cover it, but check with your LEA. Some medical schools run pre-medical courses for those who don't have an A-level in chemistry.

Tip: a final thought in looking for that course. When you go to higher education, you'll be investing several years in a course. This will cost you in terms of time and money. Isn't it worth spending the time to make sure the course is really the right one for you?

SUMMARY EXERCISES

▶ A key element in successful course choice is the research you do to make sure that the course matches your interests.

▶ Think about what you want to achieve from higher education and plan accordingly.

▶ Think about your long-term goals as well as the shorter ones.

▶ How broad do you want your studies to be?

▶ How soon do want to specialise?

▶ Take your proposed subject at university and compare three or four different courses and note how far they differ. Which is your preferred course content and why?

▶ Compare modular degree courses at two or three institutions: how do you feel about modular degrees?

FOUR

Higher education is all around you – any time, any place

Today's world demands an educated society

Learning is now a lifelong process. We live in an increasingly technical and rapidly changing society and well-educated, skilled people are in demand. World-wide, governments want to make education more accessible to all, so that the workforce can reach its maximum potential in the workplace. For its part, the educational system is trying to help the 'late developers' by making sure they have access to training and education at a time that's most convenient to them. This will increase your opportunity to study when it suits you.

Today's workplace needs people with a wide range of skills

Most industrialised countries recognise that a key to success in competing internationally is the way in which countries develop their people. Because the nature of the workplace and economies have changed, organisations are calling for people with different skills than in the past. Quality customer service is vital: it's the chief way companies are either going to win new business or maintain their current customers.

Companies and organisations are also calling out for more graduates, at least people of graduate calibre. Employers need people who can handle large amounts of complex information, who can take responsibility for a project and their work from start to finish, who can handle people (both clients and colleagues), cope with change, meet challenges, think intellectually, have enquiring, questioning minds, and keep learning. Employees also need to be responsible for updating themselves. Technology, accountability, tough competitive markets and customer demands have driven up the need for a trained, flexible workforce.

As a result, Britain has made a university education more available this century by:

- building more universities
- encouraging students to enter higher education, especially if access has traditionally been difficult for them
- increasing the range of courses available thereby increasing student interest
- increasing the range of qualifications you can enter higher education with
- enabling mature students to go back to university for a 'second chance'
- encouraging international students to study in Britain to make universities more diverse places
- encouraging universities to work with employers and the community to meet local needs in terms of training and education

'So what does this mean for me?'

- You could start work and study for a degree as an external student or by correspondence through the Open University or at evening class.
- You can study for a degree on a part-time basis.
- You don't have to do A-levels to get into most courses, although some admissions tutors still prefer them.
- You could start at one university and finish your degree at another, without repeating the work, if there is a close correlation between courses.
- In a professional capacity, you may find yourself turning to universities for training or further qualifications, such as an MBA (Masters in Business Administration) or even a PhD, perhaps sponsored by your employer.
- You have a wider choice of courses and institutions to consider.
- As an 18- or 19-year-old, you could leave going to university until later on – for example, in your 70s!
- Students attend British universities with a wide range of international qualifications, enhancing student life by their presence and encouraging international networks.

► One-third of young people aged 18 now go on to university, but many of these are surprised to find that there is a very heavy proportion of mature students studying alongside them! You can start a course when the time is right for you.

'*I want to have a year off before I start my degree*'

Many students choose to take a year out between further and higher education and there are masses of really exciting opportunities to do something different, either in Britain or abroad. This is also known as 'deferring entry' or 'taking a gap year'.

The policy towards deferring entry for a year varies not only from one university to another, but from one department or faculty to another within an institution. Check *in advance* with the institutions on your short-list to make sure they don't mind. Some subject areas prefer you to go straight on. And *don't* call it 'a year off'. It will sound to everyone that you are intending to have exactly that. Universities and employers will expect any time out to be spent in a constructive manner, doing something meaningful. The wise student plans ahead: 'Brilliant. I'd advise anyone to have a year out. I really feel refreshed and ready to get back from studying now.' The unwise student leaves it all too late, misses deadlines, gets bored, fed up and ends up doing something unmeaningful just to get through the year. 'I *told* you shouldn't have had a year off...' (parent).

There are loads of activities you can get involved with and your choice will depend on your reasons for taking a year out. Work experience will help in planning your career strategy and provide useful ammunition for later on when you're job hunting. It can also provide you with savings and possible future employment in the holidays and even after you've finished. Many employers recognise that young people want some time out between further and higher education and so are offering one year opportunities in the workplace, fully expecting you to disappear to university at the end of it. Check out the Year in Industry programme, for example. Other students prefer to spend six months of their year out working to save money before taking off to travel or work their way around the world (you can always travel later in your holidays).

Whatever your plans, make sure they'll add to the value of your CV and that you're not likely to be reducing your chances of being accepted by the university of your choice because they prefer you to go straight on after education. Plan well ahead – some schemes have a long application procedure with incredibly early application dates.

'Will this be my only chance to take time out?'

No, it won't. You can always take time out later on, for example, between jobs.

> **'**I was working in media sales. I was made redundant but fortunately I got a good package. I wanted to take some time out to think about my next move, so I used the money to spend nine months travelling around the world. You can always find time later on to take time out after your degree.**'**   Susie, history graduate, media sales

'My parents are really worried that if I have time out, I won't want to go on to HE'

Parents worry a lot about you taking a year out. They fear you may go off the idea of going to university. Sometimes, this works out well because you discover you don't want to go.

> **'**I finished my BTEC National in business studies and decided to spend a year in work before applying to uni. I got a job with Barclays and ended up staying with them. I still got to work abroad through the bank for a year, which was an invaluable experience, plus I got an MBA later, studying part-time. A job is what you make of it and you can always do a degree on a part-time basis.**'**
> Stuart, bank manager

If your parents go green when you mention having a year out, their main concern will be, will you go back? Your answer is that most students who've had a year out benefit in all sorts of ways: refreshed when they return to study, more motivated (yes, they really want to go), money saved if you've been working so you won't have to rely on them so much, plus greater maturity to cope with life there. Employers place great stock on work experience of any sort: it shows motivation. If they are worried that you'll do nothing and slump at home in front of the telly after a couple of months (supported by them), then you need to show them what you are going to do in advance. Do your preparatory research, then talk to them. Show them what you have in mind to do. They will feel much better.

'Can I go back to education much later?'

Many mature students (the term for those over 21) use higher education courses as a way to change their career by taking vocational courses or to prove to themselves that they can do it.

'You can do it: it just takes motivation, plus support from your partner or family'

Remember: it's never too late and no, you're not over the hill. Admissions tutors like mature students, because they are very motivated and committed to what they are aiming for. Many have given up a great deal to come on the course, eg, their job, and a number use higher education as a way to change career.

> 'I worked in a bank for years after leaving school, but somehow I just felt it wasn't me. Then I saw a notice in the local paper about a careers evening, so I went along and talked to a number of people from various universities. I spent some time researching my options and chose – after much soul searching and midnight discussions with friends I could trust – to do a four-year course in public relations. The drop in salary has been a hell of a shock, but I saved as much as I could in the year before I started, and that's helped. I'm surprised at the number of mature students there are – I thought I would be the only one!'
>
> Simon, mature student (43), public relations degree

'Will I cope? I'm terrified of failing the course'

Actually, some mature students find that courses move too slowly for them in the first year.

> 'The first year seems to be geared towards giving us time to settle in, which was all right for the younger students, but some of us who were a bit older found the pace too slow – after all, we are there to work and to learn.'   David, mature student, history and English

Other mature students, however, don't find the first year too slow at all, because they want to be in a friendly environment and worry about coping with the workload. Not all is plain sailing, however. Problems mature students frequently face can be isolation (because they aren't living in hall, so it's harder to get to meet people), finance (a major worry) and coping with friends and relatives who appear to think they've got lots of spare time on their hands: 'Could you just look after Jonathan for a couple of hours later today? You're not doing anything, are you?' If you can talk to mature students at the university, it's worth doing so to see what they think and how they've adjusted. Tell your friends and family that you're busy as if it were a normal working week – you're at work from 9am to 6pm or whatever. If you're married or with a partner, a lot will depend on their support. 'Women support men more than the other way round' (Tricia, doing English Lit). It's not really like *Educating Rita*, although you will find yourself changing as you go as you benefit from new experiences. And no, it's not like going back to school – it's up to you how much you do and when you do it, to an extent. Consequently, mature students do extremely well in higher education; they tend to be better organised and more motivated.

You can start university too early: normally entrants must be 17 by 1 October of the year they start their course, but others require that you are 18 at the date of admission. That said, some universities are giving special tuition to incredibly bright youngsters aged 11 or 12.

And afterwards?

Find out about the graduate market for mature students. Some employers are more prepared to take you on if you've done a relevant course – it's evidence of interest and commitment. You could:

► visit your local institution and spend time in the careers service there, to see if there's any up-to-date literature on mature students and the employment market;
► develop a network of employers early on and keep them updated with your progress; one of them may offer you a job;
► contact the Careers Service Unit for information on careers for mature graduates.

Part-time degrees

There are lots of part-time degrees, enabling you to work for vocational and/or professional qualifications at different levels, some of which are geared for people already working in the industry, such as the part-time palliative care degree at Oxford Brookes. Some universities offer a very wide range of subjects and entry qualifications will vary from one place to another. If you've got relevant experience, commitment and proof of your ability to study, you never know.

Other part-time degrees are more academic in nature – English, philosophy, French, history, biology, etc. Birkbeck College in London, all the first degrees and more advanced courses are devised to be part-time; classes are held at night outside of 'normal' working hours so you can go from work to class. You may be able to swap from a full-time to a part-time degree or vice versa depending on your circumstances and the flexibility to do so, which will vary from one course to another. Entry qualifications are normally the same as for a full-time degree and you should apply in the year before the course starts.

As a part-time student, you have to pay your tuition fees yourself, but sometimes there may be concessions so check with the Finance Office at your proposed institution.

Tips: going back to education

- ► Many universities run a service for adults and produce a mature students' guide – ring your local institution to see what they can offer.
- ► Some universities, for example, the University of Strathclyde, run summer schools for people who are a bit out of date.
- ► Some institutions run a separate test for mature entrants.
- ► In recognition that many parents want to go back to studying, most institutions run child care facilities – but demand will be heavy, so get your name down early.
- ► The hours that resource centres are open have extended enormously, enabling part-time evening students to take advantage of them.

'Do I have to do the whole degree?'

No, you don't. You may be able to enrol as an associate to pick up a couple of modules that interest you personally or which will enhance your career prospects (it's something to add to your CV). You might want to get back into study mode and prove to admissions tutors that you have the ability to study at university level, or to get a taste of higher education to see if it really is for you. If you do continue your studies, however, these modules may count towards a degree.

'Can I learn just for the fun of it?'

Some universities organise a range of courses for adults who want to study just for the pleasure of it. The University of Sunderland, for example, runs a number of courses such as 'Trace your family tree' and 'Health and fitness for the over 50s'; while Bournemouth University runs 'The Internet' and 'European affairs', among others. So go on – pick up the phone and get in touch with your local university. You never know what they've got to offer!

Learning at home

This is a growing option, but you need to make sure you're motivated to study after a long day at work. After getting in from work and having that much needed G&T, it's much easier to switch on the telly than switch in to a distance learning course. The Open University offers recognised courses you can study at home – you should do between 10 to 15 hours a week. There are no minimum entry qualifications (you can do an introductory course if you're really rusty). Courses run from February to October and consist of correspondence materials, written study texts, tapes, videos, broadcasts on the radio and TV and residential summer schools. There are tutors, counsellors and study centres to help too. You won't get the full flavour of being a full-time student, you'll need gallons of willpower ('I'll just watch Coronation Street and then I'll make a start.') and you won't necessarily qualify for a grant for tuition so check with your LEA. But you will be able to get a degree while working or you can take the units you've done and apply to enter the second or third year of a degree course full-time if your circumstances change. It depends on how far you've got. ('Well, may be another glass of wine, Jim. It might help my thinking.') Contact the OU for details (address in 'Further information'). It's ideal for people who want to enhance their careers or study for the sake of it, but also want to or have to work full-time.

The University of London runs an external degree scheme. You can sign up as an external student, sitting examinations at any one of a number of centres throughout the world (the British Council will have details). It usually takes at least three years to obtain an external degree, but you'll find comfort in the knowledge that the standard is the same as those courses taught internally at the University of London. Contact the University of London External Programme for more details (address in Further information).

Finding local, part-time or distance learning courses

Check:

- newspapers, both local and national
- your local TEC to see what is available
- your local institution; ask for a brochure
- the Open University for information
- if you are abroad, contact the British Council for information and help or surf their WWW site for details. You could study for a degree from home!

'We've got a problem at home... can I drop out for a while?'

There are occasions, particularly for mature students, when people need to drop out for a while for reasons like finance, family illness, etc. It's easier if you are doing a part-time, modular course where you study different units every term. If you need to drop out for a while, discuss your options with your personal tutor.

Moving about the country during your degree

If you may need to move institution after a year – perhaps because your partner has been asked to move locations at work – don't despair. A system called the Credit Accumulation and Transfer Scheme (CATS) means that you can take credits with you from one university and apply them to studies at another, so you don't have to repeat anything. For example, the South East Consortium for Credit Transfer involves 29 institutions within a 50-mile radius of London. This means that you can transfer credit between different institutions. In Scotland, the system is called SCOTCAT.

That higher education course could be closer than you think

You won't necessarily have to travel very far to take a course because higher education institutions are trying to bring them closer to you. The University of Lincolnshire and Humberside has arrangements which mean that locals can study at certain points throughout the county, either via a network of communications technology or through franchised HND courses at local colleges of further education.

Many universities and colleges are developing links with local institutions through compacts, consortia, partnerships, courses and open days. In some cases, courses have been franchised out to local associate or licensed colleges, even though they're in the university's prospectus. Read information about HND or HNC courses carefully. You never know. Guidelines are also available in the *UCAS Handbook* which may also alert you to franchised courses.

Local links have advantages:

- ► it's easier to find out more information, through visits, discussions with people who have contacts there, etc;
- ► you can save money by living at home, though in the case of home students this may affect your grant;
- ► it's helpful to mature students who cannot leave the area due to family, partner's job, etc;
- ► it can be a useful way to move from one course to another, through access courses, for example, where further and higher education providers meet to discuss course content, etc.

Higher education courses could be just round the corner from you – so pick up the phone and ask!

Universities are training employees

Many companies work with local universities to develop training programmes for their employees through flexible learning packages. This means that the courses are developed specifically for a group or organisation. Some courses may lead to a degree; others may lead to no qualification at all. In many cases, the background knowledge and experience of the students on the course will be taken into account, so some students may finish more quickly than others. In-house training courses and professional qualifications may sometimes contribute to a degree course, although there will probably be a fee for accreditation and validation.

Some firms organise sponsorship for employees so that they can take professional qualifications which are given degree status. This is happening in the banking world, where you can get a BSc Honours degree in financial services on completing the ACIB, if you have enough credits.

Universities may also provide short courses for business and industry, tailor-made to suit the needs of a company and staff. Interested employers should contact the External Relations office, Industry Liaison office if there is one, or the appropriate department.

SUMMARY EXERCISES

▶ Higher education is probably far more accessible than you think – so find out what's available in your area.

▶ If you're at work and you see a course that interests you (for example, an MSc in information technology), your employer may be willing to sponsor you through the course if it's relevant to your work and will enable you to do your job more effectively.

▶ What part-time courses are available locally? Check your paper to see.

▶ What are the advantages and disadvantages of studying part time and full time?

▶ Taking three or four prospectuses, check to see what sort of contacts each university has with industry.

▶ Use the Internet to find out about distance learning courses.

F I V E

How do institutions differ?

Which institution?

In Britain, higher education institutions include universities, colleges of higher education, institutes of higher education and specialist colleges (there are also private institutions). Together, they form a considerable network of teaching, expertise and research, from the Scottish Highlands and Islands right down to the Channel Islands. Geographic access has never been easier, increasing numbers of groups and organisations are turning to higher education institutions for research purposes, and TECs are encouraging local employers to tap into higher education's expertise in teaching, training and research. Many mergers and amalgamations have taken place as institutions try to make better use of their resources, forming centres of excellence. All of which makes higher education a very exciting place to be.

'What about quality in all this?'

The quality of research and teaching of many subjects within higher education has been assessed, and the results published, every three years. Any prospectus you pick up will tell you if the institution has recently been subjected to an assessment. Reports are available, either from the institution or the Higher Education Funding Council. Although they tend to be outdated rapidly, you can see for yourself how institutions that have been assessed have fared. Students are encouraged to demand more from their institutions, which means that many universities and colleges are having to work much harder than ever before. Their views are sought through questionnaires, surveys and committees at every level through the university via student reps.

Assessing the quality of the different courses

'Has this university got a good reputation?' 'Will employers recruit from this university?' 'Would it be better to have a degree from an ancient university or a new one?' These are all questions prospective students want answers to, particularly if they want a job at the end of their course. There are several factors you should take into account here:

► In any league table, somebody has to be bottom, but it doesn't mean the institution isn't fulfilling the needs and dreams of its students.
► Not every single student will be best suited by going to the universities at the top of league tables.

> '*I was offered a place at Oxford, but I turned it down and went to Exeter instead. I preferred the atmosphere. It's turned out to be the right choice, although people couldn't understand at the time why I turned Oxford down.*'   Jack, second-year law student

► There are employers who recruit from specific universities, but equally there are many who aren't worried about where you studied so much as what you got out of it in terms of skills, competencies, knowledge and potential.
► Work experience and early career planning will give you a key strategic advantage in securing employment.
► League table results are more important to some students and employers than others.
► *The most important league table is yours*, according to what you want out of an institution, a course and the life there. And the quality will depend on how much you give while you are there, in terms of motivation, commitment and making the most of the course and resources available to you.

All universities are currently subject to two national bodies: the Higher Education Quality Council and the Higher Education Funding Council; they are likely to merge. In 1993, the HEFCE started to assess the quality of teaching in universities, subject by subject, over a five-year period and these reports are available from the HEFCE. Prior to April 1995, departments were assessed as excellent, satisfactory or unsatisfactory. At any university, one department may have scored an 'excellent' while another may have been given an 'unsatisfactory' – universities don't automatically excel or just pass right across the board. After April 1995, the process of awarding these assessments has changed, now departments are 'quality approved' or 'subject to reassessment within a year'.

Current students are good sources of information. They will tell you what they think of the course, whether there is sufficient space in the library, whether the university has produced a system to overcome the problem of shortage of reading materials by computer systems management, overnight loans, short-term loans, etc. They will also tell you whether lecturers are prepared for their lectures, how much preparation they do for tutorials and seminars (and therefore how involved they want to be), whether there is a variety of teaching methods and how much the department or faculty is prepared to hear their requests and act on them, where they reasonably can.

Here are some suggested questions for finding out more about the quality of courses and whether they match what you are looking for:

- ► Does the department have set aims and objectives? Does the course?
- ► Does it review these every year, thereby giving scope for improvement?
- ► How does it take students' views into account? And employers'?
- ► How much feedback is given to students? A mark? Helpful comments?
- ► What connections are there with professionals in the area to ensure that standards are high and appropriate to real life?
- ► Is the course recognised by a professional body? If not, why not?
- ► Have the staff all got relevant training to teach? If they are teaching vocational courses, have they got recent knowledge and experience of their subject in the workplace?
- ► Does the institution concentrate on doing a few things well, or everything available not very well? For example, some universities have concentrated on delivering professional studies to very good effect.
- ► What is the staff : student ratio?
- ► What is the employment record of past graduates like? Where have they gone?
- ► What percentage of international students make up the student body? (They will make for a very diverse group of students which will only serve to broaden your horizons.)

► What are the resources like? Are the libraries well stocked, the labs well equipped and does the department have its own resources for students' use?
► How has the department (note, the department, not the university) fared in the research and teaching assessment exercises? How recent were they?

If you're looking for an institution with a department that's strong in research, check out the research assessment exercises: the results determine to an extent the resources departments will get in the future.

British higher education institutions are very diverse

Universities

► Universities put emphasis on the study of a subject or topic in tremendous depth and concentrate heavily on research. They can create their own courses and award their own degrees by virtue of Royal Charter.
► Assessment tends to be by examination plus dissertation or project.
► They offer more full-time than part-time courses, especially in older institutions.
► Most people are 18 to 22 years old.
► Most students come through the traditional A-level route, although this is changing.
► They have fewer vocational courses although they are still strong in areas like medicine, veterinary science, engineering and law.
► They have lots of research resources available: the ancients (Oxford, Cambridge, St Andrews, Glasgow, Edinburgh and Aberdeen) are all more than 700 years old!
► University buildings likely to be in town and/or on campus.

The huge red brick and civics offer a wider range of subjects than the ancients, but still concentrate more heavily on the traditional arts, humanities and science subjects than the newer universities, offering areas like classics, ancient history, Greek and Roman studies, economics, Arabic, Chinese, philosophy, American studies, plus earth sciences, life sciences, chemistry and maths. They may also run vocational subjects like engineering, medicine and dentistry, education, commerce, management science and medically related courses. Examples include:

Birmingham	Leeds	Manchester	Reading
Bristol	Leicester	Nottingham	Sheffield
Exeter	Liverpool	Queen's Belfast	Southampton
Hull			

Technological universities

These tend to:

- offer few arts and humanities programmes
- concentrate on science, technology and engineering
- have very strong links with industry and employers
- have most students doing a work experience placement
- provide courses that are likely to offer professional exemptions or student membership of organisations
- have strong employment records
- have companies coming to them offering to sponsor students
- be in the city centre or in a campus setting.

Examples include:

Aston	Bath	Bradford	Brunel
City	Heriot-Watt	Loughborough	Salford
Strathclyde	Dundee	Ulster	Surrey

Other campus universities offer a broader range of courses and have established themselves as centres of excellence very quickly; Warwick is an example. They may offer more combined courses, enabling you to do a couple of subjects at the same time under a more flexible scheme, or interdisciplinary courses like European studies. Examples are:

Keele	Sussex	York	East Anglia
Kent	Essex	Warwick	Reading
Lancaster	Stirling	Ulster	

Tips:

- Campus universities can be very convenient – everything is close to hand.
- Check to find out what links are available with the town in terms of last bus back after a night out, costs of getting to town, etc.

New universities

The polytechnics were formed chiefly through the amalgamation of colleges of technology, commerce and art and design, some of which went back to the mid-19th century. They were designated universities by the 1992 Higher and Further Education Act and instead of being assessed by an outside body, they could award their own degree programmes and plan their own programmes. Previously, courses at the new universities were validated or approved by the CNAA (Council for National Academic Awards) which assessed them to ensure they maintained standards comparable to the universities. They:

- excel in quality assurance exercises because they're used to being assessed by external bodies
- have a long experience of working with professional organisations and employers and providing professional and vocational courses to meet their needs
- have staff with industrial or professional backgrounds and this experience gives them an awareness of the needs of the world of work
- took most of the burden of expanding student numbers
- encourage those who have not entered university before
- encourage entrants coming in without traditional A-levels
- offer a range of HNDs, HNCs, professional and vocational qualifications on a part-time and full-time basis in the evenings, during the day, at the weekends
- tend to be on several sites because they amalgamated existing institutions – work out in advance which one you'll be on
- have a wide-ranging student body consisting of people of all ages.

Ex-polytechnics have not had the advantages traditional universities have enjoyed in terms of research activities, but with the publishing of the research assessment exercises, they are making a determined effort to catch up fast. Sheffield Hallam had particularly improved its research ratings in December 1996 and Westminster was recognised as excellent for its media studies research.

Examples of ex-polytechnics include:

West of England	Central England	London Guildhall
Coventry	De Montfort	Derby
East London	Greenwich	Glasgow Caledonian
Huddersfield	Leeds Metropolitan	Liverpool John Moore's
Manchester Met.	Napier	Northumbria at Newcastle
Nottingham Trent	Plymouth	Portsmouth
Robert Gordon	Sheffield Hallam	South Bank
Sunderland	Westminster	Wolverhampton
Bournemouth		

The more recent universities cover a wide range of courses, including creative and expressive arts, fine art, design, fashion, architecture, law, accountancy, business studies, management, community professionals, teaching, social work, nursing, librarianship, engineering, science, technology. They also offer arts and humanities courses, with some exciting combinations, and they have excelled in some quality control exercises. Some offer greater flexibility than others. They pioneered the systems of modularisation and credit transfer.

Other new universities serving a local need include Abertay Dundee, Anglia Polytechnic, Brighton, Glamorgan, Hertfordshire, Humberside, Kingston, Luton, Central Lancashire, Middlesex, Oxford Brookes, Paisley, Staffordshire, Teeside and Thames Valley. Check to see what the accommodation is like at the newer universities – they may cater largely for local people and therefore their housing could be rather more limited than older universities'.

Some offer very considerable listings of combined modular schemes or combined honours, so check the prospectus – they are designed to give you maximum flexibility!

Colleges and institutes of higher education (CHE)

The first thing to say is: don't confuse these with colleges of *further* education. At least 55 per cent of the students at a college of higher education must follow higher education courses. Degrees are usually validated by a university, the national accrediting body, or the institution itself. The main points about CHEs are:

- they are seen as caring, cosy and supportive places
- you get to know people quickly
- excellent support services
- many were founded by the Anglican or Catholic Churches and there is still a strong Christian way of life there – although you don't have to be a Christian to go!
- lots of close attention
- high standards of teaching – many were founded as teacher training colleges
- usually smaller than universities – some people may find them claustrophobic while others feel comforted by the size
- size can mean fewer options available within your subject area
- resources are likely to be less than at a larger institution.

Many are located in old towns such as Winchester, Cheltenham, Gloucester, Chichester, Norwich, Plymouth and Canterbury. They offer arts, design and media studies, the built environment, business professions, catering, recreation and tourism, education/teacher training, the environment, humanities, science, technology and engineering plus social and health studies.

Some colleges specialise in courses such as art and design or agriculture while others offer the full range of courses. If you are hoping to follow a serious career in an area which demands talent, then you may want to think about attending a music college, drama college or dance school, especially if you want to be a performer. Your careers service or library at school will have details of these, but you should consult with specialists in the field with a view to discussing your long-term goals as a professional. Your specialist teachers will know if you have a talent for your interest which could develop into a career. Such specialist colleges will expect to see considerable achievement in the various examinations available through different boards over and above your school work, in addition to frequent participation in extracurricular activities such as orchestras (if you play an instrument), the theatre (drama) or dance productions. Alternatively, you may decide to study all three within the scope of a performing arts courses, probably at a university or college. Note:

- everyone at a specialist college is like-minded – you won't get to meet as wide a range of people as you would in a university
- they are usually small with lots of support
- specialist colleges should have excellent links with employers

- its facilities should be totally geared up to and concentrated on one area of study: your career area of interest
- check that you'll still get a grant; you may need to find all or some of your own funding towards tuition fees at a private or specialist college.

The University of London

This incorporates 35 institutions and colleges, from Royal Holloway in the west to Wye College in the east. Whichever college you go to, you get a degree from the University of London and have access to all the services and facilities of any University of London institution. It includes institutes and colleges which have a narrower range of courses, like Heythrop College (theology), the School of Pharmacy, Wye College (agriculture) and Jews' College. Studying in London can be exciting, challenging and wonderful. There's a fantastic amount of research, teaching expertise and resources in a small area. You tend to feel as if you 'belong' to a college rather than the University of London itself. But it can be isolating and you can spend a lot of time and money getting places.

University of Wales

Another federal institution; you get your degree from the University of Wales, but each university has an identity of its own, giving students a different experience and lifestyle. You can also learn Welsh! There are several colleges of higher education, now associate or full colleges of the University of Wales. You'll find easy access to beautiful countryside; of the main universities, for example, Aberystwyth and Bangor are coastal backed by mountains, as are Swansea (coastal) and Cardiff (the capital). Lampeter, just north of Swansea, is a small university, with some 1,500 students.

Scottish universities

Four of Scotland's universities – St Andrews, Glasgow, Edinburgh and Aberdeen – are older than the English and Welsh universities, save for Oxford and Cambridge. Scotland's higher education differs from that of the rest of the UK:

- institutions place emphasis on breadth and depth of study so most courses are very flexible
- a degree lasts four years as opposed to the usual English or Welsh three-year course
- you can delay your choice of specialised subject a year (unless you're studying for a professional qualification when you have to meet the strict requirements for study for the professional bodies)
- Scotland recognises a wide variety of entry qualifications – check prospectuses
- you apply through UCAS
- degrees awarded for arts subjects are generally MAs
- you may manage to negotiate your way on to year two of a degree course.

Scottish students starting university tend to be younger than their English peers, which means that they find English courses demanding (and may benefit from an extra year at school) and that English students may find the first year too slow.

'What's a franchised course?'

Some universities have franchised courses out to local colleges of further (or higher) education. This means that the latter teach you but you still obtain the qualification from the university which has franchised the course.

You need to be careful about this, as you could apply for a course which you think is taught on a site in, say, Milton Keynes only to find it is actually being delivered in Bedford. This could alter your experience in higher education significantly. Franchising is more common with Higher National Diploma courses than degrees, but none the less it is something universities are looking at with great interest in order that they may make more effective use of their resources while providing a greater service to the community at large. For many people studying a franchised course will mean that they can live at home.

American universities in Britain

Some American universities have campuses in the UK, often close to London or in it, or in other areas with strong tourist attractions, such as close to Oxford, Cambridge or 'Shakespeare country'. They frequently advertise in the press as offering degree courses. Check to see whether their degree is awarded by Royal Charter and who approves it – if there is no Royal Charter or approval by a British university, be on the alert. Degree courses run by international universities in Britain are not necessarily recognised by employers in Britain or anywhere else, and you may need to fund the entire course yourself. If you're an international student, find out what currency a degree from there would have back home.

Two guidelines:

- ► How detailed is the prospectus? Does it lay out what you can expect from each course; the resources; accommodation facilities? If there are loads of pretty pictures and not much information on the course, be wary.
- ► If the prospectus mentions a prominent institution as willing for you to share its facilities, make sure that this is the case. Some colleges write their literature in such a way you think you'll be sitting in class alongside students from these certain prominent institutions – and arrive to find that's not quite the case. Talk to students who've been and find out if the college and course are really for you.

'From the initial course literature, it looked like we were going to be studying at the University of Zest. We got really excited, because it's such a traditional university with lots of history and a good reputation. As it turned out from the subsequent stuff we were sent, there was no actual link. The institution was merely located in Zest. First impressions gave us falsely raised hopes.'

Maria, American student seeking to study in the UK

Check affiliations carefully; if necessary, contact the British university in the same town and ask the Registrar's office for details of the connection.

Private colleges in the UK

If you need to brush up your English before starting a higher education course, note that a large number of private colleges and schools run English courses so that you may increase your word and speech power in English prior to starting your university term. Contact ARELS (see the Glossary) for information on recognised schools.

Private colleges are not funded by the British government, nor are they inspected by it for teaching quality or facilities, but they may be members of accredited bodies such as the British Accreditation Council for Independent Further and Higher Education (BAC). If a college has been accredited, it has been inspected by the Council and met certain standards set by the council on premises, organisation, control, supervision of staff and students, the quality of teaching and welfare of students. Accreditation is, however, voluntary, and although there may be some private colleges not accredited who do offer a high standard of service, you cannot be sure.

Some universities and colleges are independent of direct government funding, and they offer degree courses. Some are well known, like the University of Buckingham or the Royal College of Agriculture at Cirencester. Check the grant situation and how it would affect you well before you apply.

If you are thinking of going to a private institution for any reason, things to check are:

- The cost of the total package – tuition, fees, accommodation, food, course materials.
- That employers will recognise the qualifications you'll gain.
- The availability of resources – a small private college probably won't have the same resources as a large one, unless there are specified resources which are shared between them.

'I've seen a course being run by a British institution abroad. What do you think?'

Many British universities and colleges are developing a range of courses (distance learning, part-time, or full-time) abroad, perhaps through sponsorship or setting up campuses in other countries. If you see a degree advertised by what appears to be a British institution, get further information, *read the small print*, seek advice, and talk to previous students.

Things to think about:

- Which institution validates the degree?
- Are the teaching staff permanently resident or flown in for the odd lecture? If the latter, how much liaison is there between the course resident director and staff back home?
- Will the course be funded by your local authority or will you have to pay for tuition and everything else?

- What is the view of staff back in the home institution? Supportive? Hesitant?
- What are the facilities like? What arrangements have been made for resources such as library, computer work stations?
- Can you get access to quality reports on the course?
- If the institution claims an affinity with a British university, what exactly is that affinity?

A course which looks very exciting and promising in an advert and apparently offers lots of career opportunities could bring you to a sudden halt if at the end of it you discover that it's not recognised and you have to pay for it. Make sure you know what the full cost is before you start out – and that you know how you're going to pay for it.

'Is this course recognised by employers?'

Check *before you start* the course that the qualifications you'll get will be recognised back in your home country. Look at the small print of the marketing literature and check with sources like employers, the British Council, employment agencies, your Ministry of Education and professional organisations. Some courses advertised by British institutions abroad are not recognised by the employers in the country they have been established in.

SUMMARY

➤ You need to decide what you want out of an institution.
➤ Be wary of league tables other than the official ones.
➤ Talk to current students if you can about their experiences.
➤ Make up your own mind about what's right for you.

Does it matter to you whether your proposed institution has:

- a very high degree of mature students (eg, on part-time courses)?
- a high ratio of men to women or vice versa?
- lots of international students? The University of Birmingham for example has 1,800 students from 128 countries
- students only studying a specialist area in a specialist college or a wide range of students taking courses in everything from art to physiotherapy? What strengths do you want your prospective university or college to possess? Excellent reputation in teaching and/or research? Strong links with industry? The presence of national bodies and centres? Specialists in a certain area of study? International links and strong study abroad programmes? Check through the prospectus to see how the institutions match up to your needs.

Looking for the right place for you

You will need to decide which is the best place for *you*

This point cannot be emphasised too strongly. Never mind where your best mate is going, where your mother went or what the school thinks you should do. *You* need to decide what sort of place you want in terms of the course, the expertise, the resources, lifestyle, accommodation and facilities for sport and interests. There is absolutely no point in signing up for a place if you're going to be miserable there for three or four years.

The choice is yours

The stages to successful choice are:

- working out which subject you want to do and discussing likely exam results with subject teachers;
- identifying which institutions offer the courses you want and which offer the angle you want to do them from;
- identifying those courses whose entry criteria you should be able to meet;
- adding personal preferences, needs and values;
- making a short-list of seven or eight, weighing them up and narrowing those down to a maximum of six: most students end up with four or five really serious contenders.

It's unlikely that you'll find a place which meets all your desires and needs. But you can certainly do a lot to get as close as you can to what you want – once you've worked out what's important to you in a university or college.

'I'm a Southampton supporter, so I really wanted a college or university that was in that region. Portsmouth fitted the bill perfectly – it meant I could get to lots of home games.**'**
Jenni, computer science graduate, computer consultant

'I wanted to have the chance to go to lots of concerts – we don't get many really good groups down in Truro. Manchester is great for music – I'm hoping to stay in the area after I've graduated.**'**
Sammy, geography student, second year

People look for different things in a degree programme. Here are some of the factors which enter into choice. As you go through each one, rank them as:

essential;
important;
would be nice;
doesn't matter;
irrelevant.

Are resources important to you? If so, what sort?

Think about what you want the university to offer in terms of any art and design materials and equipment, the library and information and communications technology.
Some of the points you could look at include:

- opening hours of resource centres; the University of Bath has just opened a 24-hour library – other institutions shut at the weekends, some open late in the evenings
- technical support: to help you with video/audio production for practical course work and support for classrooms
- learning packages, to help you learn how to make the most of the resources available
- access to a departmental library, museum or collection
- the range of learning resources available
- the number of study spaces there are per university and for how many students
- the number of computer workstations there are and how many students are likely to want to use them
- the ratio of academic staff to students in the department (gives you an idea of the help you're likely to get)

- the current links with employers (local, national and international) and professional organisations and bodies, higher education institutions at home and abroad
- specialists in a given area of expertise in which you have a specific interest eg, AIDs (medicine, social work), driver behaviour (psychology), nursing mental patients (nursing), Jewish history (history).

Do you want to attend a university that has strong links with research units and institutes? For example, Bournemouth University has strong links with the National Centre for Computer Animation, and the Centre for Culinary Research.

Student support

If you require special support, some higher education institutions will be more appropriate for you than others. Identify the help you need because specialist staff will need to know very clearly what your difficulties are so that, together, you can work out whether theirs is the best university for you. Visit the institutions on your short-list, especially if you have mobility difficulties, so that you can see exactly what's what.

Invest time in talking to students in the same boat as you – they can show you how they are meeting their needs and explain what help they've had. Universities may be able to give you support such as extra time in exams, a personal helper, student readers, adapted accommodation, extra support materials and extra tutorials if you have learning difficulties. Also, additional financial help may be forthcoming from other sources, so talk to your careers adviser or careers teacher.

Some students need more support than others in terms of the opportunity to discuss progress with a tutor. Find out what support is available through the personal tutor system and how effectively it works. The National Union of Students reports that students often complain that the personal tutor system is close to collapse in some institutions. However, some students don't feel the need to talk to their personal tutor throughout the entire time they're at university.

'I didn't see my personal tutor after our first meeting when I arrived in October, not for the three years I was there. But then, I didn't need to see him so there wasn't any point.'
                    James, physics student, now working in research

If you think you are likely to need close, personal attention, try to assess how the system is standing up to student needs.

Get the facts on the universities you are thinking of applying for, such as:

- their methods of teaching
- group sizes – in a large group, the lecturer will not know students so well and be less likely to help if you've got problems
- how the personal tutor system works, for example how many students is the tutor responsible for?

How do you want to be assessed?

A course which is assessed by a number of methods will give you the opportunity to develop skills you may need at work. Many courses will give you the chance to present material using audio-visual equipment to a variety of audiences, lead seminars of ten to 20 or more students, managing a project which has perhaps been presented to you by an employer, from start to finish. You'll find yourself writing reports, essays and possibly dissertations, organising and participating in exhibitions and trying not to blow the place up in laboratory practicals. Then there will be the old familiar exams system, where the phrase, 'You may now turn over the paper' makes you feel sick with excitement or nerves.

Mature students may find their previous work experience and qualifications are sufficient to contribute to at least part of their degree. Some courses will assess you constantly through a whole range of coursework, while others will rely on both coursework and exams. Of course, you may prefer to leave all your assessment to the end via exams.

Think about your preferred methods of assessment (do you enjoy exams or avoid whenever possible?); talk about these with your teachers or tutors and check prospectuses or with individual departments to find a course which will match your preference.

'I want to gain skills employers want in the workplace. Help!'

It's difficult to assess what the employment market will be like in three or four years' time, but there are things you can do to give yourself a strategic advantage when it comes to looking for work.

Get skills in information technology – especially if you have a phobia of computers
Employers want computer-literate graduates. Most courses will encourage their students to become competent in the use of computers, either through including IT teaching or making sure that self-learning modules in the resource centre are available. The University of Sunderland offers an IT for All Scheme: you can take modules at different levels of studies in a wide range of IT topics. You may just want to pick up a couple of units in IT to grasp the basics. You should have an understanding of how IT can be applied to the workplace.

If you're doing a vocational course, do you want one that offers exemptions from professional exams and/or student membership?
Professional organisations lay down the guidelines for education, training and qualifications for their members and many universities offering vocational courses that have strong links with the relevant body, so first degree and HND courses will share much of the same material.

Some (but not all) degree courses lead to exemptions from professional examinations, saving you a stage or two when you arrive at work and start training – the relevant professional body should have a list of recognised courses in the UK or you can check individual prospectuses. At Aston University for example, as a managerial and administrative studies graduate, you can claim useful exceptions from all foundation examination subjects of the Institute of Chartered Accountants and some of the written exams for the Diploma of the Chartered Institute of Marketing. Apart from anything else, this shows commitment to a career area – something employers like. You've got a jump start and got ahead.

Some courses may also enable you to become a student member of societies and professional bodies. for example, if you were to read combined honours chemistry at Aston University, you may become a student member of the Royal Society of Chemistry, and you may be able to progress on to higher membership grades. This could give you access to employers coming to do presentations, newsletters, job vacancy listings, etc.

'If I'm doing a vocational course, how do I know that I'll be taught the sorts of skills and knowledge an employer needs?'

Since many professional bodies lay down guidelines (strict or not) for course content, if you're heading to achieve professional exemptions, the courses should be similar. But if universities and colleges are to equip students with the sorts of skills and knowledge employers want, there must be a strong link between universities and employers as individuals and professional bodies. If you're looking for a course with strong employer involvement, you could ask:

- How do employers and/or professional groups get involved in the course? Do they contribute to its planning?
- Do they contribute to the delivery, for example by giving lectures?
- Do they take part in assessments by, for instance, listening to presentations by students?
- Which employers get involved? Are they local? National?
- How much contact with the professional organisation is there?
- Are employers involved in departmental policies and planning?
- How much social contact is there with employers? Hull university's accountancy department and social organisation arranges socials, bringing students and accountants together informally.
- Does the course apply knowledge to the workplace or a working environment?

You may find your course work gives you the chance to work on 'live' projects, put forward by employers who need work done. Some universities use local TECs to find employers who need research done, thereby matching students who need to complete a dissertation with the employer.

Do you want to actively profile your skills throughout your course?
Employers want to recruit students with a range of strong transferable skills including interpersonal skills, business awareness, team-working, self-management, planning and organising events, analysing abilities and communication. Institutions are developing programmes whereby you can profile your skills. Oxford Brookes University presents you with a record of achievement when you leave, which you can show prospective employers. The University of Lincolnshire and Humberside degree programmes include units called 'Transferable skills' to help you find your preferred learning style and develop the skills and capabilities useful for employment, further study and training.

Get a strategic advantage... do a sandwich course
A sandwich course involves time away from the university, either

studying abroad or gaining work experience. Most students will take a year to do the 'sandwich' part of the course; some do two six-month placements instead, normally in the summer term and holidays. Some universities offer work experience as an option regardless of your degree discipline. All students at Brunel take part in work experience, gaining them valuable strategic advantages when it comes to job hunting.

A typical course may run like this:

Year one   University course
Year two   University course
Year three   Work placement/study abroad
Year four   University course.

Many courses offer the option to leave out the work placement or study abroad experience; this is particularly helpful in the case of mature students who may feel they already have considerable work experience under their belt or who may have lived abroad already. However, it's worth bearing in mind that many work placements lead to a job offer.

Questions to ask about sandwich courses include:

► Who finds the placement – you or the department?
► What resources are there for finding placements – specialist staff who will help you; staff whose job it is to find the placement?
► How is the placement monitored and assessed?
► How are you assessed?
► What happens if a placement cannot be found?
► Is the placement optional?
► Which companies have taken on students before?
► What did final year students who've just done work placements think of them?
► Will your local education authority support your year in industry?

Pick up work experience through schemes not necessarily related to your degree
Recognising the value that employers place on work experience, many universities are offering students the chance to do something different between their penultimate and final years, such as going off to teach children in a school in South America or conservation work in a Brazilian forest. (OK, they're just examples.) The year will have benefits.

‘It was a maturing experience.’

‘I now know I want to teach primary school.’

‘I was going to be a teacher, but now I know it's certainly not for me – thank God I found out in time.’

‘I was really refreshed by the time I returned to my studies.’

Check prospectuses for details.

Do you want to study abroad?

Students who study abroad generally enjoy the experience and benefit from it. In a world where it's not unusual for business people to fly to Hong Kong for lunch ('important PR to go'), spending part of your degree abroad makes for good experience.

Universities have responded well to student requests for more opportunities to study abroad, through study abroad programmes, acquiring 'partner' institutions and exchange agreements which operate between universities world-wide. Exchange schemes normally mean that you don't have to pay any extra tuition fees and international or European offices help sort out your accommodation, visa applications, and credit transfer back to the UK.

For example, Sheffield Hallam's School of Financial Studies and Law runs a BA (Hons) financial services and *Diplome/Maitrise en Banque – Assurance* with the Universite de Caen in Normandy. When you graduate from Sheffield Hallam, you are also eligible for a *Diplome* or *Maitrise* from Caen University!

The European Union is constantly seeking to increase student and staff mobility, hence SOCRATES. This initiative incorporates ERASMUS (study abroad), LEONARDO (work experience) and TEMPUS (Central and Eastern Europe) and funds are available to students on these programmes. It also means you can pick up a qualification from another university.

Most students will take classes at a foreign university, sitting alongside the home students, or act as teaching assistants in schools for a year, or do a placement with a company.

Here are some points to check:

- ► What sort of contact is there between your home university and your institution abroad?
- ► How are you monitored and assessed?

- What support system is there while you are abroad? Will you cope?
- Is it compulsory or optional? Can you make up the experience by any way other than taking a full year, eg, working during three summer holidays?
- Are you limited to going to specific towns or cities abroad? Can you set up your own programme?

Studying abroad can be a lot of fun, but you may well find there's far less individual support and personal attention from your university there. This can prove to be very stressful: but remember that it's during the bad times that you most develop as a person!

Do you want part-time work opportunities?

Some universities have their own employment agencies which may find you part-time work within the university or with local employers. Sheffield Hallam University runs a part-time employment bureau called Pronto; the University of Greenwich a JobShop. Part-time work means you can boost your finances, gain useful skills and network with employers and employees – people always know of employers who are recruiting. Your time management will need to be excellent but you will help your budget and develop skills you can use at work. It may even land you a full-time job after you graduate. *You never know.*

'Where shall I study in Britain?'

Well, wherever you go, it will be wet and cold most of the time. So the weather shouldn't be a factor. You could study in your home town or region, move away from home to a university or college somewhere else, or study your entire degree abroad.

Studying at home means it may be easier to find part-time work as you'll have an established network of family and friends. It could be cheaper and easier to study because you won't always have your friends banging on your door shouting, 'We're going down the Union... come with us. Do your reading tomorrow.' You could also study part-time or do a distance learning course from home while working. You won't have to lug great cart loads of luggage around the country at the start and end of term. But you'll get a reduced grant, possibly less independence and more interference in your new life from your family, plus you'll need to establish new ground rules with your parent(s) for going out and so on.

Moving away from home enables you to get deeply involved in the total university experience. It could be easier to study as you'll have your own study room – or not, depending on your motivation (writing up a practical or going to the night club?) You decide how you want to spend your day with no interference from anyone save the timetable. And you'll get used to moving from home, which could prove easier when you look for work; you'll already be used to being thoroughly independent. If you want a part-time job, you'll need to start building up your network of contacts again. It could be more expensive than living at home (all that socialising and buying alka seltzer), it could waste more time ('I was so hung over today, I didn't get up until 3pm.' – and that was Monday). Plus you've got to get there – which costs, although there are lots of good student deals around. It's up to you, but hitching isn't a good idea – you may never arrive.

If you want to study abroad, you'll probably relish the experience of living and studying in another country, learning about a different culture and acquiring an international network. You could, however, do a distance learning course and stay at home, so check. Obvious disadvantages of studying abroad include the cost, plus your qualification may not be recognised by employers back home.

Tip: you're not alone if you study at home. According to the Higher Education Statistics Agency, in the 1995 entry, nearly half of the students studying full-time courses did so in their home region.

Looking at studying in the UK

How is your UK geography? British institutions are located all over the country, in towns, in the countryside, by the sea.

Tip: find out more about the area around the universities you are applying to from the local tourist information office. It will tell you lots about the region, the town, facilities, accommodation, and economy. A town which relies on tourists could lead to problems in the summer when your accommodation is needed for B&Bs.

Your surroundings

Do you want a change from your current lifestyle and scenery? Maybe you live inland and you want to experience life by the sea for once. Perhaps you're dying to try out a sport like mountaineering or caving, or want to live in a huge city as opposed to a small village with access to galleries, museums and concerts. Maybe you're fed up of city life and want to try something smaller, where you can feel part of the community quickly.

Many of Britain's cities and towns offer access to outstanding areas of scenic beauty. If your general knowledge about Britain is sketchy, get an atlas and do some research. Britain's geographical areas differ tremendously and one may suit you better than another.

Does size matter?

It matters to some people. Would you be happiest in:

- a large city with lots to do, especially in terms of galleries, theatres, plays, shopping, and nightlife or
- a smaller town where life will be quieter?

Each has its own pros and cons. Large cities may appear to have lots of cheap accommodation, but you'll be competing for it along with the unemployed, homeless, and low income families. If you go for a town or city where there are lots of student colleges and campuses, there will probably be more student facilities for you to make use of. Loughborough, for example, has 20,000 students from four institutions.

Large universities may be broken down into units known as 'faculties' so that while you are a student at the University of Wolverhampton, which has 23,000 students, you study in one of five faculties, each specialising in an area of study on a different site. This means that you have the benefits of a large institution but are located in a faculty which is almost like a small university on its own.

Smaller universities may be friendlier places, where it's easier to get to know people and where you may find that you have more attention and there's more time for individuals. It may be easier to fit straight in; you'll get to know more students well and settle down more quickly. St Mary's University College, for example, has 2,200 students: everyone knows everyone else and new students settle down quickly. But your options and facilities may be more limited compared with a larger institution. You may find that larger places, though they have lots of facilities and more choice in terms of courses, may be more impersonal. People react differently to size and it's up to you to weigh up the options and how you feel about the advantages and disadvantages.

Getting there and home again

It's pretty easy to travel around the UK, thanks to rail and bus services and there are always good deals for students – 'Make the most of them while you can' says one graduate enviously. Taking your luggage with you at the start of your university experience is exhausting, but shouldn't determine your course choice!

Living near relatives

Do your parents want you to study at the University of Glasgow because Great Aunt Bertha is there and they feel comforted by the fact that a relative will be near to you when you leave home? Or do you want to be at the other end of the country to Great Aunt Bertha and your relations? Being close to relatives means, 'I can always have access to a good meal.' They, however, may not keep their distance, popping in at the wrong times. Overseas students coming a long way from home may find it a comfort to be close to relatives or friends in Britain.

Location of the university in town

Some universities are right in the centre of town, the mathematics department being just round the corner from the High Street, which means that you're more likely to feel integrated with the town. You might live a couple of miles from your lectures and have to spend time getting to class every day. You may prefer a campus setting, just outside town. Check the frequency and cost of bus or tram services to and from the university and town.

Living on campus will be lively, and you'll spend a lot of time rolling out of bed and strolling straight to lectures and then on to the Union for a coffee or a pint. Campus facilities generally include a cash point, a bank, supermarket, travel agency, sports complex perhaps and, most importantly, a cheap bar. Check how far the accommodation is from campus if you move out of halls in your second year.

Does accommodation matter to you?

Many universities have improved their accommodation facilities to match increased student numbers and to cater for conferences and holiday touring groups in the vacations. Standard student accommodation usually offers several options: single or double bedrooms in a hall of residence, either en-suite or with wash-basin and shared bathroom facilities; a common room where you can sink into comfy chairs and argue over which TV channel to watch; small kitchens for you to fix a light snack in, and possibly laundry facilities. Some may even have their own library or bar. Halls could be mixed or single sex and there's usually a catering plan so you're paying for two meals a day (breakfast and supper) and it saves the hassle of thinking about what you're going to cook. If you're a late riser, however, you may find yourself missing out on breakfast a lot and meal times could prove restrictive in the end. You can save money by sharing a room but think about the sort of room-mate you would be willing to share with (smoker who plays loud music all the time, or non-smoker who likes the quiet life?) Plus sharing a room can intrude on your nocturnal activities in all sorts of ways ('God, he snores'... yes, well).

Student flats/self-catering halls offer single study bedrooms and you share a kitchen, lounge and bathroom with several other students. There are usually a variety of places to eat on campus, but they can be costly even though they're subsidised. You may all find it's cheaper to buy food in bulk and take it in turns to cook. (Could be risky – see what everyone produces for the first few weeks on their own.) There could also be problems if you've got someone who's apparently never heard of the words 'washing up'. Self-catering is a useful option if you can't get up in the morning and hate being restricted to meal times.

Tip: buy a cookbook for students to get some cheap but nutritious recipes.

Whether you're in a hall or self-catering accommodation, they provide great ways to meet other people – and there's always someone around for a chat.

Lodgings are an alternative source of accommodation if you can't get into halls. You either live with a family or get a bedsit. The accommodation office should have a list of respectable places for you to visit – most have been on their lists for years. You may get bed and breakfast alone or dinner thrown in as well. You either pay the landlord directly or to pay the university which reimburses the landlord or family. A pro is that your landlady may turn out to be a real trooper (does your ironing, brings you tea when you're hung over) and if you're an international student, living with a family can be comforting and an excellent way to experience British family life. The main con is that it's harder to meet other students – you have to make much more of an effort, especially at first.

Tips for overseas students

► Some universities stick all overseas students together in a block, which may make it more difficult to meet British students. If you definitely want to be put in a block with the locals, let the accommodation office know.

► Many universities and colleges make overseas students a priority when it comes to housing.

► Don't send your family to Britain until you have organised their accommodation.

► Housing for married students is very limited – don't bring your family to Britain unless you have accommodation for them.

The Accommodation Office will keep a register of private housing in the area; they may even visit as many as possible to assess their suitability. They may also be able to help students wishing to change their accommodation or who are having problems with finance, rent, contracts and disputes with landlords. The Student Union is also a helpful contact.

Some points to bear in mind are:

► Will you be renting your accommodation for the whole year or the academic one?
► Sort out your accommodation *before* term starts.
► How much it will cost you – in time and money – to reach campus/class facilities from where you're living?

If you have special needs, contact the universities concerned to ask their advice and visit institutions to check out their suitability and see how they can be adapted to suit your needs.

Make use of student guides, alternative prospectuses and the university prospectus for universities you are considering applying to so as to get an idea what accommodation is available.

Does cost matter to you?

If it does – and it will to most students – there are several sources you can check to find out which places are the cheapest to live in. *The PUSH Guide* is a mine of information on this subject – it even includes the cost of a pint of beer in the Union bars or in the city or town. They also give indications of the cost of accommodation (your major expense) in the first year in hall and private accommodation outside it. In particular with regard to cost, you should check:

► Travelling expenses to get to the university and, once you're there, to get to lectures and back.
► The cost of accommodation after the first year.
► Whether the institution are going to introduce top-up tuition fees (it must mention this in their prospectus) – at the time of writing, some institutions are considering taking this action.
► How carefully you can budget your money – are you naturally cautious or slack?
► Whether your course will demand any extra fees for course equipment or field trips, etc.

► How much help the university can give you in finding part-time employment to supplement your grant.
► How much you would save if you were to share a room.

Compare costs between different institutions (including tuition charges if you're an overseas student) and weigh these up against the other factors you deem important in a course. A lot will depend on your budgeting skills and how resourceful you are!

What can you do in your spare time?

Do you have any specific interests or hobbies you want to start or continue at university? Most student unions have loads of clubs and societies which organise events, talks, meetings and outings throughout the term. Some institutions have better sports facilities than others; one may have a sports teams *par excellence* who do battle on the university's behalf in British Universities Sporting Association (BUSA) competitions; others will have teams for those who want to bully off, have a bit of a knock about and then head for the bar. Some students look for institutions which will get them involved in the Officer Training Corps, Air Squadron or Royal Naval Unit. If you're a keen golfer, you may want to seek universities which have good golf courses close by. A small number of the Royal and Ancient Golf Club Bursaries are available to full-time students at the University of Strathclyde (based, one should add, on golfing merit).

SUMMARY EXERCISES

▶ People have different ideas about what they want out of a university course; what matters is what's important to you.

▶ Think about the sort of institution you want. It's important to be happy if you're going to spend two, three or four years in a place.

▶ Make use of all the information available to you to do your research. And visit if you possibly can.

▶ Rank all the factors in order of importance as suggested at the start of the chapter: essential, important, would be nice, doesn't matter, irrelevant. Compare your list with a friend or a group of friends. Discuss reasons why you've all made up your list in the way you have.

▶ Look for institutions which meet your needs, starting with those you ranked 'essential', by reading individual prospectuses, using ECCTIS, surfing the Internet, talking to past or current students, and visiting.

▶ Come up with a short-list of seven or eight to research more closely.

Applying for courses

Looking at the time-scale

Currently, the application system to British higher education works in such a way that you narrow your choices down from:

1. All the universities and colleges offering higher education courses within the UCAS system at the start of your search for the right course for you.
   To:
2. Up to six courses to list on your application form by 15 December in the year *before* you want to start your course, ie, roughly nine months before you start and well before you know the results of any exams you are sitting in preparation for higher education. If you are applying to Oxford or Cambridge, the deadline is 15 October and note there is a dual route for applying to some art and design courses (more on this later).
   To:
3. Two choices by the summer before you start –
   (a) your firm choice, ie, 'I want to go *there*'
   (b) your insurance choice (your 'just in case' option which usually requests lower entry grades than your firm choice).
   To:
4. 'This is where I'm going – I've got the grades they wanted', in mid-August when exam results come out and places are confirmed; or '*I haven't got a place – I need to go through Clearing*' (more on Clearing later in the chapter).

Eighteen months pass between your thinking about higher education, determining which course is right for you, applying and actually starting.

UCAS

Almost 418,000 students applied for a place in higher education in Britain for 1996 entry; 295,818 were accepted. Students apply through a centralised system, namely a body called the University and Colleges Admissions Service – UCAS. It administers the applications for all *full-time* first degrees, diplomas of higher education and higher national diplomas for all students. For the benefit of the reader who hazily remembers organisations called UCCA, PCAS and ADAR, well, they've all merged to form UCAS.

UCAS also provides clear and accurate information to those applying for higher education and their advisers, together with a wide range of advisory services for them. In this way, careers advisers and counsellors are kept up to date with new developments and changes to the system. You would be well advised to listen extremely carefully to any sessions delivered on the application process. Applicants make too many mistakes in the application process because they don't listen or think carefully enough!

How does the application system work?

You send your application form to UCAS; UCAS sends photocopies of your application form to the institutions you wish to apply to. Those institutions decide whether to offer you a place or not and let UCAS know their decision. UCAS will pass on decisions as they receive them and then send a summary statement with the last decision. It's at this point that you are asked to identify your firm (first choice) and insurance (second choice) acceptances.

All applications for entry to all stages of the courses listed in the *UCAS Handbook* must be made via UCAS, unless you are transferring to another course within the same institution or at a different UCAS institution.

What can't UCAS do?

UCAS plays no role in the selection process itself. That is entirely a matter for the institutions you apply to. Each institution can decide its own admissions policy. The number of places available for students from the UK and EU will depend on the allocation of state funds made by the Higher Education Funding Council. Financial penalties may be imposed on those institutions which fail to meet the targets set, either through over-recruitment or a lack of students. UCAS cannot therefore intervene on your behalf to argue a rejection response. While overseas students are outside this quota, even if they meet the entry requirements demanded, it may be that space in a laboratory or practical area prevents an offer being made. Selectors' decisions are entirely up to the institution you're applying to. If you want to argue their decision, take it up with them, not UCAS.

What you'll need to apply

- An application form.
- Instructions leaflet which explains fully how to complete the form. Read it with care.
- *UCAS Handbook* which lists institution and course codes and provides details of the application process itself.
- Acknowledgement card.

These are available from:

- Your careers teacher (if you are at school or college).
- Your local careers advisory company or careers service.
- Your local British Council office.
- UCAS itself. If you write to UCAS from outside the UK, you will need to send £5 sterling, payable to UCAS, to cover the cost of postage and packing.

For entry in 1997, it costs £12 to apply (£4 if you apply to one institution only). The instruction leaflet gives full details about the application fee.

You should also take note that, although you can complete a written application form, UCAS has introduced an electronic application form. Ask UCAS or your careers teacher for more details.

When do you need to apply?

A reminder of the vital dates:

1 September – 15 October   Applications for Oxford or Cambridge
1 September – 15 December   Applications for everywhere else.

The earlier you complete your form and get it in, the better. It must reach UCAS in Cheltenham by these dates. Schools and colleges may have an internal deadline of their own for you, so that they can get the references done in good time. They will tell you if they do.

If you are a mature student on an Access course, the likelihood is that the 15 December deadline will be difficult to meet. If your Access course has strong links with the university or college you want to go to, it's less important to meet this deadline. If it hasn't, you're best to send your UCAS form in anyway with the supporting material later. There are special notes for mature students, available from UCAS.

Applying to Oxford and Cambridge

You cannot apply to both in the same year unless you wish to apply for an organ award at both universities (see the Glossary). If you are applying to either, you must apply through UCAS and also make a direct application. Details of the application procedures may be found in the *UCAS Handbook* and the prospectuses of both universities.

Tip: beware of advice. Lots of people may try to give you advice on a system that has changed considerably even in the last year. For instance, 'in the old days', you put your choices in order of your preference. *Now* you put them in the order they appear in the *UCAS Handbook*.

'What about the Diploma of Social Work and Nursing courses?'

Currently, students applying for undergraduate programmes apply through UCAS where the Diploma of Social Work is awarded with a degree or a Diploma in Higher Education. Otherwise, students apply through SWAS (see 'Further information' for the address). From 1998, UCAS will also manage the application process for all nursing and midwifery courses via NMAS (Nurses and Midwives Admissions Service).

Your application form is your marketing tool

Your application is crucial because, for many courses, it will be your only chance to market yourself.

Picture the scene. You're an admissions tutor at a very popular university and you've been inundated with applications for your course. It's up to you decide who to offer a place to and who to reject. It's late at night, you just flew back that morning from an international conference in Los Angeles where you had to deliver a paper on your area of research. You pick up your 700th application form for your course since 1 September. You reach for your stone-cold cup of coffee, knowing that you've still got another 20 forms to look through before morning. What can a candidate do to make you sit up and take notice of an application form?

There are a number of things admissions tutors look for in your application. Make it as easy as possible for them to read and you will start scoring marks straight away.

Thoughtful presentation

If you've taken time to complete the form, it will show. Write legibly or type. The form will be reduced in size making it harder to read at the best of times; if you've got very tiny handwriting, this may become virtually illegible on the form as it is reduced, so make it a bit larger than normal. Write in black ink or type the form so that it photocopies well – blue ink rarely comes out clearly.

Make sure you have not made any spelling or grammatical mistakes. And don't send in a form that's smeared with coffee stains or marks from a can of Pepsi. Make your original a clean, sharp version. Blurred, illegible, badly written application forms riddled with spelling errors are enough to annoy any admissions tutor. You must get the form right first time, so:

- *Take a photocopy and practise filling in the form first*, so that you can work out how you're going to use the space on the form; this will pay dividends.
- Read the instruction leaflet very carefully. Fill in your photocopy of the form as you read the instructions, section by section.
- Be honest. You should be able to talk about anything you write on your form, especially if you are interviewed – your interviewer may be an expert on your favourite hobby!
- Don't attach anything to the application form. If you really want to send something (for example, because you are a mature

student and you think your CV would help the selectors), ring the appropriate department's admissions tutor or secretary and ask if you can send it on separately with a covering letter.

Before you are parted from your application form:

► take a photocopy and kept it in a safe place – if you are interviewed, you can remind yourself of what you put on the form;
► sign and date the form;
► get it checked by an adviser;
► give it to your referee.

Specifying your choices

You can apply for up to six choices – you don't have to use all six. If you want to apply for more than one course at the same institution, then you generally make a separate entry for each choice. If, however, you are applying for a degree *and* HND in a shortage subject like science, engineering or computer science, you could apply for the degree. If you're applying for a more competitive area like business studies, talk to your adviser and only go for the degree if you're likely to get the required grades. If you do well on the HND's first year, you could always see if you can transfer to the degree course.

When you fill in the application form and list your choices, you'll be asked for a number of codes, listed in the *UCAS Handbook*. For example, if you were to study a Business Studies degree at the University of Hertfordshire, the codes would be as follows:

Institution code name: HERTS
Institution code: H36
Course code: N120
Short form for the course title: BA/BS

The instruction leaflet and *UCAS Handbook* explain how to complete the section where you should indicate your choices, but if you are stuck, get advice. Failure to complete it correctly means that consideration of your application will be delayed while the mistake is sorted out. This could mean you're rejected or a higher grade is asked of you.

For each of your choices, make sure you have the right qualifications

Check first *The University and College Entrance: the Official Guide* before moving to the prospectus and any departmental literature again for an indication of the standards sought for the qualification you are applying with. Check also that you can meet any specific needs for GCSE subjects and grades. If you don't have a specifically required qualification but think that a course or unit you have studied in further education may cover similar material as an alternative, talk to your course tutor and consult with the institution's prospectus to see if it might cover you. Make sure that your referee knows what you are planning: see if they will support this strategy for covering a weakness in your reference.

Admissions tutors want to see that you have the ability to succeed

That's why they'll look at your examination results: (a) to show that you can stay the course and (b) for proof that you can do well in academic exams. They'll also look closely at your reference, in particular to what your referee says about your study skills, academic strengths and interests and likelihood of succeeding in higher education. If you're a mature student who bombed at school, recent serious academic study will give you the chance to get your study skills going again and prove that you have the ability to complete the course.

Admissions tutors want to see evidence of interest in your proposed subject (and career)

This is where Section 10 of the UCAS form, the all-important Personal Statement, can make such a difference, especially if many students meet the required entry criteria for a few places. You've got to convince the admissions tutor of your interest in the course and why you want to do it and, at the same time, show him or her that you'll be the sort of person who'll gain a lot from the higher education experience and give a lot back. They want to recruit people who are going to contribute something to university life, so show them that you don't just spend your free time sitting at home watching TV.

You may well wonder, 'How can I fit this all in and make my writing legible?!' Take a piece of paper and pen and do some rough work first. If you have a Record of Achievement (current students or recent school and college leavers only will have these), use this to compose your thoughts. You will need to show:

- why the subject appeals
- what appeals to you about the courses you have chosen
- evidence of interest in the subjects you propose to study
- proposed career intentions (if known) and how you have found out about them eg, work experience (expected for most vocational courses) or at the very least talking to professionals, spending one or two days with them, visiting places of work, reading trade magazines
- why you want to enter higher education
- how you have taken advantage of opportunities eg, through Young Enterprise, work shadowing, careers conventions.

Your evidence of interest, such as visits to museums, art galleries, plays, the theatre, experiments at home, building models, etc., depending on the course, should not be confined to classroom activities. At university, you'll be expected to do a great deal of studying and work on your own through your own motivation, so you should be able to show that you have these abilities through out-of-the-classroom activities.

Will you add sparkle and life to the university?

Anything that shows you can undertake responsibility and get involved in things helps. Universities want to admit people who are going to mix well (ie, work well with others) and make the most of the opportunities available to them throughout their life at university – to get stuck in and fully involved in student life as opposed to spending three years locked in their bedroom with a set of books. Your application form should show that you like to make the most of the opportunities open to you and how involved you like to get, so give them an idea of the extent of your hobbies. If you go swimming once a term for the fun of it, it doesn't really count. If you train daily with a team of swimmers, this shows greater commitment and involvement. You don't have to produce a list of hundreds of things you do, just two or three will suffice.

Admissions tutors differ in the ways in which they like to see Personal Statements completed, but many won't object to clearly laid out statements in which you have headings and bullet points underneath them, like this:

10 PERSONAL STATEMENT

<u>Why apply for these courses?</u>
I want to study equine management because... (Say why the course appeals.)

<u>My research into these courses</u>
I found out about these courses by... (Show that you've done some research into the courses and how you did it. Mention also any employers you've had contact with if you're applying for a vocational course so that you can show you understand the implications of your career choice, eg, 'I spent a week with a racing stable in Yorkshire which gave me the opportunity to talk to trainers and the year lad about careers in the racing industry.')

<u>Work experience</u>
For the last ten years, I have spent every weekend at the local riding stables assisting the instructor. (Explain what you did. Mention anything you've done in work that's relevant to your course.)

<u>Qualities I have that will benefit me in HE</u>
(Say something about your abilities to work, motivation and commitment, and your personal qualities, so that they get an idea of the sort of person you are.)

<u>My interests</u>
(Comment on these both in and out of school or the workplace; mention any responsibilities you have or membership of any committees and teams. If you put 'reading', be specific, eg, 'I enjoy reading books by Dick Francis, Jilly Cooper and John Francombe'. Try to show how involved you are in any activities and interests.)

You can then emphasise points which they – weary and on their umpteenth application form – may appreciate with speed. Think about the course you're going to do: if you are applying for a subject in which your ability to write fluent English is important, such as English literature, you may be better sticking to prose. One fine art applicant completed his statement through a series of cartoons; he was successful but not all art and design admissions tutors will welcome this approach.

Any personal circumstances affecting your studies? Let them know!

If you have suffered circumstances which have affected your studies and consequently may impact on your results, such as a family bereavement, illness, attack or any other disability, let the university know. This applies after your application form has gone in, too. Some admissions tutors may take this into account when your results come through. It is particularly important that you answer the 'disability' question honestly so that the institutions concerned can check that the special support you require can be prepared for. They won't discriminate against you so long as they can provide proper provision.

Tips: writing personal statements to 'sell yourself' is never easy so:

- make notes first, to decide what you want to include
- plan the order in which you want to write your statement, eg, what appeals about the subject first, hobbies later
- use the summer holidays to practise writing the personal statement
- show it to a careers officer, sixth form tutor, adult education adviser, etc
- once you have written the personal statement, leave it several days and go back to it – you'll look at it with fresh eyes.

Is your application supported by your referee?

Who will you ask to act as a referee? If you are studying at a school, the headteacher or head of sixth will normally provide the reference – ask. If you're at college on any course, your tutor is probably the best person to act as your referee. Get your form to your referee as soon as you can in the autumn term.

'A lot of students come to us a few days before the 15 December deadline, expecting us to suddenly produce first class references for them and to get their forms posted off in time. The end of any term is always a very busy time for anyone in education, as there is a lot happening: so my advice to any students seeking references is to get your form in well before even mid-November. It gives us time to write a reference that will really mean some thing and genuinely help the admissions tutor.' Head of sixth form

Remember that while 15 December is the deadline for UCAS forms (save Oxford and Cambridge), it also falls ten days before Christmas, so it's naturally a busy time for everybody, be they admissions tutors or referees. Consequently, December is never the best time to hand over your application form. Think ahead.

Time it right and increase your chances

According to UCAS, some 35 per cent of the total number of applications arrive with them in the two weeks leading up to 15 December and are therefore likely to reach the institutions concerned in mid-January. Common sense says that admissions tutors will probably spend more time on the fewer applications they receive up to, say, November than those which arrive in a waterfall of paper in January. Plus they may demand higher offers in January than they might in October or November, especially if they have made countless offers in the autumn term and are suddenly conscious that they need to keep an eye on their numbers.

Mature students: getting a reference

If it's years since you were at school, you need to find someone who can act as a referee, such as an evening class tutor if you're taking an advanced course. 'What about my employer?' some mature students ponder. If you've got an employer who wants to sponsor you through a degree programme, then it would make sense to get him or her to write a reference, although first preference must still be for someone who can comment on your academic and intellectual abilities. If your employer has no idea that you are planning to go to higher education, you need to think again. Professional people who know that you've researched higher education, and can attest to your commitment and your ability to succeed might be the answer, especially if they've gone through a university course themselves.

'I'm applying for art and design courses'

Students seeking to apply for art and design courses must complete an UCAS form. You have two routes open to you and you can apply for both. The courses and routes are shown in coloured boxes in the *UCAS Handbook* entry for each institution.

Route A

These courses are identified in the *UCAS Handbook* by the suffix 'W' in the course code. You have up to six choices and you can apply between 1 January and 15 December, but you would be well advised to apply by the middle of November, because the institutions you apply to will need to organise a portfolio inspection. Your application will be considered simultaneously by the institutions listed on your form. If you are applying to do fine art at the University of Oxford, you should apply by 15 October and you need to submit your portfolio by 15 November. You can obtain further details from the Oxford Colleges Admission Office, Wellington Square, Oxford OX1 2JD.

Route B

The dates for application are from 1 January to 24 March. Because of the time available for interviewing and portfolio inspection, if you are going through this later application route you should indicate your interview preference on a separate Interview Preference Form. Applications are considered sequentially in interview preference order. If you're applying only through Route B, note that you can only hold one offer and no insurance.

You'll be notified by the universities and colleges concerned of your portfolio inspection and interview arrangements, unless you are applying to Oxford. Colleges within Route A have a central inspection scheme administered by the University of Reading and this scheme covers the fine art courses at Reading, Aberystwyth, Edinburgh, Lancaster, Leeds and Newcastle upon Tyne.

If you are applying for courses through both routes, you can apply for a maximum of six choices, of which at most four may be through the later route. Read the instructions for completion of the UCAS form and tick the box in Section 3 to indicate that you will later apply for some courses via the later route, if this is the case. UCAS will send you additional documentation later so that you can add your choices for consideration through the later route.

The fee for applications is £12 whether through Route A or Route B or both, with a reduction to £4 for a single choice.

Deferring and taking a year out

If you want to defer a year, make sure *in advance* that your chosen institutions will accept deferred entry applications (they don't have to). You will also need to make sure that you acquire any specified entry requirements by 31 August in the year prior to your starting the course. If you are offered a place through deferred entry, you cannot reapply through UCAS a year later.

If you choose to take a year out, you should sort out your choices and application form before you leave Britain if you are going abroad and check whether you are likely to be needed for interview before determining any travel plans. Leave one sensible person at home in charge of opening your mail, and agree to keep in touch where possible so that you can deal with any queries which they cannot respond to on your behalf.

Are you in full-time work already?

If you work and you hope your employer will sponsor you for a course in the *UCAS Handbook*, you should apply through UCAS as usual. If, however, you only want to apply to one institution, you or your employer could contact the relevant department first.

'I'm applying to do a part-time degree'

Apply directly to the institution. Contact the Adult and Continuing Education office if there is one, or Admissions Office, and they will advise you accordingly.

Applying from outside the UK

Apply through UCAS: follow the instructions carefully which are enclosed with the application form. British Council offices will generally be happy to give you advice on completing the application form. Again, take a photocopy of the form and practise completing it before you fill in the original; get both the copy and the original checked if you can.

The overseas students' offices in London for Cyprus, Guyana, India,

Luxembourg and Thailand (addresses under Further Information) require their nationals to submit their applications through them.

'I'm coming to Britain for only part of my degree'

If you are a student from the European Union going through SOCRA-TES or a similar exchange programme, apply directly to the university concerned through your own International Office.

If you are an American student, your application procedure will vary according to the way you are coming to Britain. If you are coming under the auspices of an American college, you may need to apply to them first. If you are hoping to do a Junior Year Abroad scheme directly with a British university, you should contact the International Office for an application form. Your Study Abroad office should be able to help.

Absolute essentials for all applications:

▶ Take a copy of everything you send UCAS or institutions directly and keep it safe.

▶ UCAS will send you a personal application number. Put it somewhere safe, where you cannot possibly lose it.

▶ If you change your address at any stage after sending in your application form, you must let UCAS know at once.

▶ Be sure you'd be really happy to go to *any* of the choices you put on the application form. Strictly and legally speaking, you cannot change your mind about your choices after applying.

'Help!'

If you need help in completing the form, ask your careers teacher or course tutor for assistance. You can also get advice from your local careers service or, for overseas students, British Council offices. UCAS offers a helpline service (01242 227788) and for the hard of hearing, a minicom text phone service on 01242 225857.

What happens to my application after UCAS has received it?

Once your form has been sent to UCAS, UCAS sends you an acknowledgement card. The acknowledgement letter takes longer depending on when the form is received. In September to mid-November, this will probably take two or three days, but obviously the delay builds up as UCAS receives more forms. This letter will give you your UCAS number. *Do not lose this number.* Make several copies of it and fix them to things that you cannot possibly lose, such as the fridge. When you now call either UCAS or any of the institutions to which you have applied, they will ask you for your number before anything else. You should also check the letter to make sure that your choices have been recorded correctly. UCAS will also send an 'Advice to applicants' leaflet, which you should read and keep safely.

UCAS will photocopy your form and send it out to the institutions to which you have a applied. The institutions will decide whether to offer you:

► an unconditional place (ie, you're in – usually for people who took a year out/are mature students/in work, etc who already have achieved the results they'll need)
► a conditional place (ie, we'll offer you a place provided that you get these grades next summer – these are the fixed grades you need to aim for)
► a place on a related degree course or a lower course such as an HND
► a rejection.

UCAS will tell you of the institutions' decisions and you must then reply via UCAS to any offers which have been made by universities and colleges – in fact you don't have to do this until you get your last offer. If you receive an offer from a place you really want to study at (it's your outright favourite), you could accept it and equally you could decline any that are made before you have received all the decisions. You cannot change your mind about any decisions you make.

UCAS will send you a 'Statement of Decisions' which outlines where you are in the application process with each institution you have applied to. You have 14 days to respond to it, although you can delay your response if you still have an open day visit at one of the universities to attend. If this is the case, let UCAS know.

The UCAS letter is the official communication and if it conveys an offer, a contract is established between the institution and you, the applicant.

If you accept a conditional offer (known as a CF for conditional firm) you can also have an insurance offer (CI – conditional insurance) so that you now have two possibilities out of your original six choices. Generally your CF will demand higher grades. The CI covers the 'just in case' scenario, eg, you had a row with your boyfriend the night before, you feel rotten on the day, the wrong questions came up, it just wasn't your day, etc. You cannot change your mind about these choices after you've made them – so think carefully.

If you don't bother to let UCAS know what you are doing in terms of accepting offers, UCAS can't hold your offers in the system – it will have to let them go, so make sure you get forms filled in and returned to UCAS by the appropriate day. Otherwise UCAS will simply go back to your six institutions and decline any offers it was holding for you on your behalf.

Similarly, anything left blank on the 'Statement of Decisions' form will imply that you are declining that place, so if you just accept one place by accident and forget to put in your conditional insurance choice, all other places will be declined by UCAS on your behalf.

UCAS will then send you a final statement of your replies and decisions; the main thing from there on in is to work hard to achieve the desired results.

'They want me to go for an interview before making a decision. Help!'

Most universities don't formally interview students because of the sheer numbers of applicants, unless they are legally required to interview prior to making a decision, such as for teacher training courses. Some incorporate informal interviews into open days, giving you the chance to decide whether the university is for you and the university the chance to decide whether you are for it. Research the course and the institution before you go. Think up some questions before your interview. If you get all the answers you want during it, you can always say, 'Thank you, we've covered everything I wanted to know.'

If you are asked for an interview and you don't turn up without letting the institution know, the university or college can send UCAS a 'withdrawn' decision – which means your application for that institution is cancelled.

Here are some tips for survival.

- Don't be surprised if the interviewers put you under pressure. They want to see how you react and how well you can debate your point.
- Read your application form prior to the interview to remind yourself of what you put and be prepared to discuss everything, including your career plans for the future.
- Don't lose your temper, shout, get aggressive, swear, pick your nose, chew gum, bang the door on the way out, gaze at your watch or out of the window.
- Make eye contact with all the interviewers.
- Smile, be friendly and positive.
- Don't blame others or circumstances for your past failings.
- Be ready to comment on issues of the day surrounding your course.
- If you don't know an answer, say so. Don't try to waffle your way out of it – you'll get found out. If you need time to think about an answer, say so: it shows you're considering your response.
- Many academics have not had formal training in interview techniques. They may ramble, waffle, argue, go off the subject and on to a tangent, not give you a chance to ask any questions… so expect the unexpected.
- If you are studying an art and design course or anything with a creative element, you'll be asked to take a portfolio of work along and be ready to discuss it. Get help from your subject teachers in preparing your portfolio.
- It's OK to be nervous.
- If your parents go with you to the interview, arrange in advance to meet at a suitable point – a coffee shop, say – some time later so that you concentrate on the interview and not on whether you will be running late to meet them. Give yourself time to reflect on the interview before you meet them.
- The departmental secretary will be able to tell you how long the interview should take. If you can't make the appointed time, call well in advance and see if it is possible to re-schedule. If you don't plan to attend, let the university know – they could give your slot to someone else who needs to change dates.
- Dress smartly rather than sloppily. Save the fashion statement for when you've got in.
- Use the interview as a chance to have a look round and talk to current students.

The rest of the summer

Stay at home from mid-August on

You will be far too busy preparing to go anywhere on holiday. If things go well and you know you have the grades you needed, you'll want to celebrate with friends and get organised for going. If you meet the grades specified by your conditional firm offer, they have a contractual obligation to take you. And if you have not got a place, you'll need to go through Clearing.

Going through Clearing

Clearing is for those who did not receive any offers earlier that year or declined all the offers that were made to them; for those who held conditional offers but failed to meet the required grades so they have no place; and late applicants who sent their forms to UCAS after 30 June during the year in which they intended starting their course.

Don't leave finding a place to your relatives, best friend or your helpful next door neighbour

Clearing should not be done for you by fond parents, doting grand-mothers or helpful neighbours for two reasons. First, admissions tutors are not impressed when your parents call because you're off doing something else. You'll need to sell yourself over the phone and to get answers to questions you may have. Second, your relatives could enter you for the course they think looks terribly interesting and which makes you cringe. Or you could find that you've been signed up in part of the country you least want to be in, even though you told your mother tearfully on the reverse-charge phone call from your trekking holiday in Spain, 'I don't care where I go, or what I do… just find me a course…' It isn't fair to leave such an important decision to others. Be there to sort it out. It's your future.

'But I'm at work all day'

A tricky one. If you're a student who is working between leaving school or college and actually going to university, explain to your supervisor what has happened and ask to have time off. University helplines have extended their hours considerably, many being open over the weekends, plus you'll still have access to careers literature in public libraries, newspapers, TV programmes offering advice, and the Internet if you're on it. In my experience as a careers adviser, many mature students who were at work and whose employers did not know they were trying to go to university – well, umm, they suddenly developed flu.

What you'll need

If you don't get a place and need to go through Clearing, UCAS will automatically send you a 'Clearing Entry Form' with instructions through the post. If you decide not to go to university that year, let UCAS know that you are withdrawing from the system.

You'll also need access to:

- ECCTIS (available at careers services, your school and college, British Council offices).
- Newspapers – *The Independent* in particular provides a very good service.
- A telephone for calling prospective universities which might offer you a place.
- Your academic details and personal UCAS number.
- Internet, television, information technology, teletext, all of which provide useful information, but are not essential.
- Impartial advice from careers advisers; it does help to talk through the options with someone.

You could also take a look back on the previous year's vacancy listings when you are making your initial choices. If a course was looking for students then, they will also probably be short the following year and will probably be pleased to receive an application.

And remember, don't panic.

"Don't panic." That's what all the careers advisers say. So tell me, what else am I supposed to do? It's like they're asking people on a sinking ship to stay calm when they're running out of life-rafts.
Scott, maths and physics A-level student, seeking a course in maths

Stages for surviving clearing

- If your grades are close to what was required, call the university to see if they will still accept you. Be prepared to do a sales pitch over the phone. If your firm offer won't, call your insurance.
- If you are rejected by both your firm and insurance offers, reassess your options (see below) with careers advisers; think broadly and start looking for suitable courses.
- Find vacancies from the sources of information listed above (this is where you start if you were a late applicant or have just decided you want to go to university).
- Find something out about those courses which demand the grades you have acquired.
- If they look appropriate in terms of course content and your personal needs, call the admissions tutor.

'Students calling us for a place should have a good idea of what the course involves at our university; they should have done some research. We also expect them to be able to tell us why the course appeals and why we should offer them a place. It helps if they appear to be organised on the phone, polite and business-like, with their results in front of them. It is very annoying when a student has to spend ten minutes hunting through a cupboard for her GCSE results. They must do a sales pitch, be enthusiastic and want to do the course. At the same time, it's important that applicants ask any questions they have about the course and that the people at the university end try to answer their questions as fully as they can.'
Admissions tutor, life sciences department, giving advice to students

- Complete the 'Clearing Entry Form'. Read the instruction sheet carefully; if in doubt ask.

Think calmly

There's loads of help and information available, mind boggling though it may be in your anxiety to find a place. Careers staff advise you not to panic while it seems your world is falling down around you. Calm, collective thinking seems like an impossibility. Your parents may be flapping around putting pressure on you to 'Sort your life out. Look, what about this course?' Even if you get a place, there's accommodation to organise. Visions of students camping in tents spring to mind. Your friends have done well and got what they wanted and they are now trying to be helpful and supportive. Meanwhile, you have *The University and College Entrance: the Official Guide* in one hand, the newspaper in the other, thinking, *'Why* has this happened to *me?'* and 'How on earth can I get out of this?'. Every day seems like a nightmare, because it's hard to see any way out. Take comfort from those who've been through it: it does sort itself out.

> 'It was awful waiting for the results to arrive. When they did, I just couldn't believe my results – they were nowhere near the BBC I needed for Hispanic Studies. I cried for hours and finally got myself over to school to talk to my careers teacher. Eventually, I got a place to read Spanish and business studies, and actually I'm enjoying the course and I'm looking forward to a year in Spain working for an organisation out there. At the time, you just feel as though there's no future – but believe me, there is.'
>
> Anna, second-year student, Spanish and business studies

There are other liferafts to climb on to. You do have a range of options open to you, including to:

- go for a joint honours instead of a single one
- look at HNDs instead of degrees
- do a different subject
- take a year out and re-take your exams (get advice from the school – if they think there could be a significant improvement, go for it; if not – is it worth it?)
- take a year out and do something different while having a rethink – all experience is useful.

Tips:

- The more flexible you are in terms of location and lifestyle requirements, the more likely you are to find a place through Clearing.
- Keep checking information on vacancies – Clearing lasts until early October.
- Check the course content to make sure that you are going to be studying something you want to study – don't grab any course and think, 'Oh, that'll do – at least I know where I'm going'. Remember, you're signing up for a three-or four-year course.

- Ignore panic headlines in the press. Remember, editors want to sell papers. Bad news sells. Concentrate on yourself and what you want.
- Universities advertise places because they want to fill them.

Go to university when it's right for you

Don't apply for university just because your friends are and your relatives and school think you should. If you're to invest two, three or four years of your life in higher education, you're not being fair on yourself if you start off with a less than enthusiastic and wholehearted reasoning for going. Go because *you* want to go.

'I couldn't go. I just froze with fear'

Some students decide not to go to university or withdraw for all sorts of reasons, including a sudden fear of leaving home or a feeling that it just isn't right.

'I'd always been keen to go. But three weeks before I was due to start an Italian degree, I froze with fear and just knew I couldn't go through with leaving home. I withdrew from UCAS, found local work and studied at evening classes. Telling my parents and the school was the worst bit because I was terrified of letting everyone down. I was in a terrible state when I told my mum – crying and shaking. She was very good about it though. I may go in the future.'

Sally, intended course: Italian

'My circumstances at work suddenly changed'

Mature students often find that they hit last minute changes of mind.

'I applied to university to do information technology. I was fed up with work, my job seemed to be going nowhere fast and I wanted a change – I was bored out of my mind. Two months before I was due to start the course, circumstances at work changed considerably. I got far more responsibility and a section to manage; I decided to give work another year and look at part-time courses instead.'

James, supervisor, shipping firm

Let UCAS know of your decision

If you decide not to go, let UCAS know as soon as you can; your place could go to someone else.

'I'm late! I missed the 15 December deadline. Can I still apply?'

Yes, you can but note that:

- applications received after 15 December and by 30 June – 'late applications' – are forwarded by UCAS to the institutions you have listed for consideration at their discretion. Thus a place with lots of vacancies to fill is likely to look at it; one which has been inundated with applications is not. Mature students should note that some admissions tutors may keep a couple of places for them; overseas students may also have more chance of getting in after the deadline, but these are very general comments and will vary from course to course;
- applications received between 1 July and 20 September are processed through Clearing; you are sent instructions on how to go through the Clearing system and can also contact your careers service for assistance.

There is also a system called 'Late registration' for those who apply after 20 September. You complete a pre-numbered UCAS form which is supplied by the university or college. And there's no fee.

The future

The higher education scene is changing rapidly and a major revision of the application system is being considered by a working party, in particular whether the system should be altered so that students apply *after* they know whether they have acquired the necessary entry requirements. This is a proposal at present and it would take some time to implement, but it does reinforce the fact that when you apply, you must have the most up-to-date *UCAS Handbook*, application form and instruction leaflet. Using your brother's copy of the *UCCA Handbook* found in the attic when your mother was clearing it out won't do.

+ help

SUMMARY EXERCISES

▶ Ask for help and advice when you need it.

▶ Keep copies of everything you send and receive in safe places.

▶ Allow plenty of time for applying – don't rush your application.

▶ Read everything that comes through from UCAS *carefully* – it will answer many of your questions without your requiring further help.

▶ What will you contribute to the universities you have chosen to apply to?

▶ What appeals to you specifically about the courses you have chosen?

▶ What evidence can you supply to show that you do indeed have a passion for the subject(s) you are about to study?

▶ You have chosen to study oceanography with geology at the University of Southampton. Using the *UCAS Handbook*, find the institution's code name and institution code and the course code. How would you write the short form of the course title on the UCAS form?

E I G H T

Money: Making an investment

When you sign up for a degree course, wherever you are from and wherever you are doing your degree, you're not just investing time in your future. Money will be required as well. While most students end courses in debt, graduate vacancies and salaries are *rising*.

Tuition and fees

These vary, depending on whether you're a home student, a student from the Isle of Man and Channel Islands, or an overseas student. Tuition fees also vary according to the course you are studying. They are higher for clinically based course like medicine than the classroom-based variety.

For British students, tuition fees are generally paid directly to your institution by your local education authority. Students from the EU who meet the residence requirements generally pay the home fee rate, although there are occasions when your fees may be paid by the British government.

Overseas students from outside the UK are normally expected to find their own fees and tuition. Overseas fees are listed in the prospec-tuses so check – and remember that these charges change annually. Usually, fees must be paid in full at the beginning of the year although in some cases it may be possible to pay in instalments. Some institutions may offer scholarships or bursaries to overseas students so ask the department or International Office.

You can't get a mandatory award or loan for part-time courses (except for some initial teacher training courses), postgraduate courses (bar initial teacher training), nursing courses under the Project 2000 scheme, courses in further education, or correspondence and distance learning courses. However, some institutions may be prepared to negotiate payment of fees. You may be able to get your employer to sponsor you, if your course is particularly relevant to the workplace. You may also be able to apply for a Career Development Loan (CDL) which may support courses in vocational subjects. CDLs support full- and part-time courses plus distance learning if it is related to a job (not necessarily a current one), doesn't last more than two years and is not supported financially by a mandatory grant at a publicly funded higher education institution. If the course lasts more than two years, the CDL will support the first 24 months. Get a free booklet by calling 0800 585 505!

Grants

Mandatory awards for UK students

Local education authority (LEA) mandatory grants cover your tuition fees and will go some way towards paying your living costs throughout the year, excluding the summer holidays. (This latter bit depends on how much your parents earn.) To get a mandatory grant, you must be accepted on to a designated course (a full-time or sandwich course leading to a first degree or a higher national diploma) and have been ordinarily resident in the United Kingdom for three years prior to the course beginning. Grants for British students have not kept up with inflation, causing the average student to finish their degrees well in debt – but it all depends how you want to spend your money and what you want to spend it on.

A tip for parents
Even if you son or daughter is unlikely to get a maintenance grant because of your income, you should apply to the LEA so that tuition fees can be paid. Otherwise, you could end up with an extra-large bill. This also applies to students from the Channel Islands and the Isle of Man, who could end up with an even bigger bill as their fees are different to the normal 'home' student.

Discretionary grants

If the course you're taking is not a 'designated' one or you can't meet the requirements for a mandatory award, you could apply for a discre- tionary grant from your LEA. Do this as soon as you can. For more information on this whole area, get the pamphlet *Guide to Students* available *free* from your local education authority.

Other sources of finance

Student loans

Currently, loans are available in Britain as a 'top-up' to a standard grant and designed to supplement living costs. The amount of the loan varies depending on whether you are living with your parents while studying, studying away from home in London or studying away from home out of London.

You are eligible if you are a UK resident attending a full-time higher education course. The system does not take into account the amount your parents, partner, spouse or other relatives earn. Contact the Student Loans Company for an information leaflet (see Further information).

Bursaries

These may be available for some courses so check with the appropriate department.

Sponsorship

Information about sponsorship is given in Chapter 2. Overseas students may be able to find an organisation which will sponsor them to get a degree and then return to their home countries with their new-found knowledge and skills in leadership and managing others.

Scholarships from your institution

Some institutions offer entrance scholarships to students; check the prospectus for further details. Employers are sometimes interested in offering sponsorship of some kind to students on highly vocational courses; ask your department for information.

Charitable bequests

You may be able to receive a grant from a charity or group which allocates funds to a particular kind of student or a course. Check *The Directory of Grant Making Trusts* in your local library. If you're a Scottish student, ask the Scottish Education Department for information about the Register of Local Endowments.

Parents

Many parents help their offspring with living costs through the years at university. Talk to your bank or financial adviser to see whether they can suggest a suitable savings plan.

Help for overseas students

To enter the UK as an international student, you must show the immigration authorities that you can pay for your fees and living expenses. This should also cover any family members you are bringing with you. If you don't have this proof, you will probably be refused entry to the UK.

There are very few scholarships available to you; contact your own Ministry of Education or Education Department to ask for details of any schemes funded by the British government. Talk to your nearest British Council which will have details of any scholarships schemes. Check the small print of any scholarship carefully, because once you are in Britain, you will probably find it impossible to get extra funds.

If you run into problems:

► talk to your adviser or your tutor
► contact the Student Union and/or the welfare officer
► talk to the International Office.

Don't try to fix things on your own because they could affect your immigration status.

It may be possible to ask the institution if you can pay your costs over a period of time instead of all at once. Private trusts and charities are normally restricted to final-year students who are about to finish. If you are waiting for funds from abroad and are stuck meanwhile, it may be possible to receive some money from public funds under the Urgent Cases Regulation – check with your adviser first.

Banking in Britain

Banks are dedicated to helping you through services such as advisory leaflets, student advisers (in some cases on campus), free banking, a cheque book, free overdraft facilities and telephone cards. Get information on what they all offer, compare them and make your choice.

So what are your costs while you're at university?

Accommodation takes up the major part of your budget and costs differ throughout the country, so find out likely costs by checking the prospectus, asking for lists of suitable accommodation in the area and consulting student guides. Check out what happens to accommodation costs after the first year, since most students in halls of residence are living in subsidised housing and the price of private housing could rocket after you leave hall and are on your own. Don't forget that as well as rent, if you're living out of halls, you'll probably have to pay for heating and lighting, water, gas and electricity as well.

In halls, fees are due at the start of each term.

You may need to pay for extra and necessary course fees such as field trips, magazines and trade subscriptions, creative art materials, computer disks, photocopying and stationery. You may need to budget for travel, not only to get to the university from your home town, but getting around once you're there. You'll need to budget for expenses such as: laundry, clothing, stationery, any food not provided in your hall of residence, socialising, belonging to societies and clubs, outings, coffee in the student bar, toiletries, buying spare rolls of loo paper for when it runs out at weekends in the hall, getting about, going home, calling home, writing letters to friends, clothing, shoes, stamps, applying for jobs, and finding out about vacation work through writing for information. And then there are the musts, like insuring all your gear.

Be resourceful

Your finances will depend in part on how resourceful you are and how well you manage your time and cash. Some golden rules are:

- don't blow your money in the first week on drinks – spread it out
- don't shop for food when you're hungry – you'll spend much more
- shop around – you'll quickly find the cheaper deals

- buy in bulk – it's cheaper
- set yourself a certain amount of money to spend every week and try to stick to it.

> 'In the first two weeks, I spend £100 going out. We went out every single night. It was brilliant, really good – I met loads of people and stuff. But now there's still four weeks to go to the end of term – and I'm overdrawn. I wish I'd spent less money in the first couple of weeks. It's too late, now, though.'
>
> Steve, first-year student, environmental studies

'You can get rid of your overdraft in the holidays by working'

You can't claim social security benefits during the vacations, so try to find a job instead. However demeaning you think the job is, it will help your overdraft and show employers you've got motivation and stick-ability and resourcefulness – all qualities they like. It will also give you an insight into what life is like at the bottom – all helpful for when you have staff to manage!

To find work, you could:

- sign up with an agency and ask for temporary work
- surf the Internet
- register with PeopleBank the Employment Network, which often has employers contact it for people to work for them for a short period of time
- sign up with the campus employment agency if there is one
- check local papers
- try local supermarkets, shops, bars, restaurants, pubs…

If you are a student from the EEA or EU, you can work without permission – you don't need to obtain any documentation. Generally, overseas students cannot work.

'You could always get a student loan – whether you need it or not – and invest it'

Now, there's a thought.

Getting into difficulties

If you do get into financial problems, don't panic. Take action early on.

> 'The envelopes started to appear and I just knew they were from the bank. I didn't dare open them so I stuck them in a drawer and pretended they weren't there at all. One day in the Union, we were talking about money and a friend told me how helpful her bank adviser had been when she'd got into difficulties. I can't tell you how much of a relief it was to go and see mine – although I was embarrassed. They helped me straight away.'
>
> Carol, second-year botany student, looking to go into research

Talk to people who can help and have experience of working with students in a similar boat. Set about working out a solution sooner rather than later – with advice from people who know what they are talking about, eg, student advisers at your bank and welfare officers. If you can show your bank you're doing something about your finances, like hunting around for work in the summer to pay off your overdraft, they will be far more sympathetic.

Access/Hardship Fund

This is made available by the government to give limited support to students on a full-time or sandwich course who are suffering real financial hardship. To apply, you must be a home student and have taken out a student loan for the current year, if you are eligible.

Looking to the future

Like higher education everywhere else in the world, it's very costly to fund considerably increased participation in university education. Sir Ron Dearing has been appointed to try to fix the mess as it stands. Suggestions have been made by all political parties as to how they would deal with the issue, and some institutions like the London School of Economics have taken matters into their own hands. Some are thinking of introducing top-up fees, where the student would have to pay an extra £1,000 or so a year for tuition. If an institution does this, it would have say so in its prospectus – so watch the press and read prospectuses carefully.

SUMMARY EXERCISES

▶ Your grant will go further than you think if you are resourceful and careful with your spending.

▶ Get advice from second- and third-year students about how they managed to cope.

▶ Check out the *PUSH Guide to Which University* to find out costs.

▶ Compare accommodation costs at a number of different universities throughout Britain.

▶ Get details on grants from your local educational authority and have a good read or start gathering information from your local British Council office to see what details they have on sponsorship or scholarships if you're an overseas student – it's never to early to start looking.

▶ Check with individual banks and building societies to see what they have to offer students. How do they compare?

▶ Check out the availability of scholarships for your proposed course of study.

Made it! Coping with student life

Getting ready

In all the excitement and inevitable apprehension that arises with the publication of A-level results, there's lots to do. Stay at home after mid-August and use the time to celebrate with your friends, make sure you have their addresses at university and return promptly any forms the university or your local educational authority send you. Confirm to your LEA where you're going to study, and what and how long the course is. Your university will probably send you a book list and information for your arrival – where you should go and what you should do. The accommodation office will probably be in touch with you as well.

Take copies of all communication between you and your institution and LEA; plus your national insurance number and tax forms, and your passport and birth certificate (for applying for a loan).

Tip for mature students with children: many universities will have some facilities for child care so check the prospectus. Facilities may include a vacation club, play groups and day nurseries. Crèche facilities are in demand, so sign your child up as soon as your can.

Read the information from the accommodation office carefully so that you take the right things with you (for example, will you need to take your own bed linen?) Most universities and colleges send out a pack to you with lots of information such as the date when you should turn up, so read it with care. If you've any questions, give the appropriate department or office a call. Take photos from home of family and friends to share with your new-found friends and things you can use to make yourself feel at home: posters, a favourite teddy bear – yes, lots of students take them under the guise of 'This is Homer. He's my lucky mascot.' Work out how you're going to get to the university from home: train, bus, car (yours), lift with your parents. If you buy a ticket in advance, you may be able to get a cheap one.

Driving to university. 'The car will be useful in the term'

Find out *in advance of your arrival* what the parking arrangements are like – spaces may be restricted to university staff and disabled students.

Cars *can* be useful for:

- getting your gear to and from college without having to lug it on the bus or train
- going to the supermarket to stock up with larger items and save money
- giving lifts to other students who want to go to town/class and thereby
- making lots of friends and using gallons of petrol.

But then cars also cost money to run and insure.

Arriving

Tip: the British Council runs a 'Meet and greet' service at Heathrow, Gatwick and Manchester International Airports to help overseas students attending subscribing universities when they arrive.

'What will it be like?'

Many halls of residence will ask you to arrive on a specific day. The first 24 hours are exhausting. For a start, there's probably been an emotional build up to your starting university, especially if you're leaving home and saying goodbye to family and friends. You're on your own now, starting a new chapter in your life! Deciding what to take and trying to pack it in such a way that you can lift it – let alone carry it – takes strategic planning.

When you arrive in the town you're studying in, the Student Union may have arranged for transport from the train and/or bus station on a frequent basis to the main sites of university accommodation. Get to the hall of residence or wherever it is you're staying. Keep your accommodation details close to hand – you may need to show identification to the porters and warden. You'll lug all your precious belongings down endless corridors which smell of disinfectant, perfume or aftershave or both, and last term's lasagne, trying to stop your baggage getting caught up with everyone else's. You'll make conversation with people you've never met and if your parents have come with you, they'll tentatively try to start chatting with your new next door neighbour. Have some coffee or tea or whatever ready to hand in your luggage plus some biscuits – it's surprising how hungry and thirsty carting around suitcases, cardboard boxes which keep falling apart, or rucksacks makes you feel. You'll probably then spend hours making idle chat with your new neighbours and trying to work out how to fit all your worldly belongings into the tiny wardrobe. If you're stuck for something to do after that, help other people with their luggage as they struggle to find their rooms, knock on doors and introduce yourself – you're all in the same boat. The phone lines will be manic the first few nights you're there; but at least standing in a queue is a good way to meet people.

If you're staying in a hall of residence, there may be an introductory meeting called by the warden to welcome you and to lay down the rules designed so that you can all live in perfect harmony. Whatever you do with your stuff, make sure you've easy and fast access to something to wear at 3:00 am when the fire alarm goes off and you all have to get out of the building in your nightwear. However embarrassed you are, if you're with a partner, take him or her with you. If it is a genuine practice – and they do happen at that hour – fire service chiefs don't take kindly to finding nocturnal partners hiding in your room and waiting for you to return.

If you're not in a hall of residence but in digs, you'll need to make an extra effort to meet people. Seek out student activities and meetings to meet people; once classes start, it will be easier because you can always ask the person sitting next to you to join you for a coffee afterwards or see if you can join their group in hall for a drink in the evenings. Everyone asks the same questions in the beginning: 'Was this your first choice, then? 'What course are you studying? What A-levels did you do? Where are you from?'

Pick up your grant cheque if you get one, usually from the Finance Office. Lots of grant cheques are late arriving – don't panic, but let the people who want money from you (eg, for rent, etc) know. You may need to open a bank account and will probably receive lots of offers from banks about the sorts of student accounts they have and all the goodies they have to offer. Weigh up all the advice and the options and decide what's best for you. You could always open an account before you go.

New students arrive a few days before everyone else so they can find their way around. There's usually a programme of events with talks by the powers-that-be to welcome you and remind you to make the most of your university days (yawn, yawn).

Freshers' week, organised by the Student Union to help you settle in, offers you the chance to get acquainted with the many clubs and societies on offer. Don't be bulldozed into joining (it will probably cost you); be selective. Finding your way about will wear your feet out and when you get back to your room, tired, thirsty and wondering what is for supper, there's the inevitable stacks of leaflets shoved under your door with news of events and offers. Don't chuck them all in the bin without at least making sure they are not important. Overseas students may be given an 'induction and welcome course' which could last for two or three days, courtesy of the International Office. You can guarantee there'll be hangover after hangover, and loads of late nights. Take painkillers with you. Be prepared.

The musts

- Get your belongings insured. Don't take valuables to university. Leave them at home. Your things may be covered by your parents' insurance – check it out.
- Register with a doctor when you arrive – don't leave it until you feel ill. The Student Union will be able to give you a list of local doctors.
- Register with the Student Union, faculty, department, library, etc.
- Pick up your grant cheque and pay your accommodation fees.
- Pay your tuition fees if you need to.

Managing your time

Everything is strange at first. Freshers' week or the Intro week or whatever it's called, will keep you busy, hung-over and tired. You'll get your timetable. Now is the time to plan so as to make the most of your university days. If your institution runs a study skills or time management course, take it. You'll fit far more in (including, perhaps, a part-time job).

Make up a timetable (similar to the sort you used to get at school, only yours will now include the weekends and won't stop at 3:30). Put in all the things like labs, lectures, seminars and tutorials that you should be going to. Make a note of exactly what work you'll be expected to do for each of your courses – your tutor should give you specific information about this at the start of the term. Add in times for reading, preparing seminars and writing labs or whatever. Work out what you want to do at university outside of academic work and add it in; for example, if you want to get involved in the community, take part in a play, etc. Once you know the timings your group will meet, stick them down. Your timetable could end up looking something like this:

	Mon	Tues	Wed	Thurs	Fri	Sat	Sun
9:00		Lecture	P.S.	Tutorial	P.S.		
10:00	Lecture	P.S.	Seminar	Tutorial	Lecture		
11:00	Lecture	P.S.	session	Tutorial	Seminar		
12:00		Lecture	P.S.	Tutorial	session		Pizza bar
1:00	Lunch	Lunch	P.S.	Lunch	Lunch		Pizza bar
2:00	Lecture	P.S.	Football	Lecture	Lecture	Football	Pizza bar
3:00	P.S.	Lecture	Football	P.S.	P.S.	Football	
6:00	Food	Food	Food	Food	Food	Food	
7:00	Football	Pizza bar	Social	Pizza bar	Social	Social	

P.S. = Private Study

This student:

► has nine hours of lectures a week, two two-hour of seminars, plus two two-hour tutorials
► has almost 20 hours of private study a week
► plays on the football team and is on the committee (Monday evenings, meetings once a fortnight)
► part-time job in a pizza bar to supplement his income
► socialises well, several nights a week
► left Saturday mornings and Sunday mornings free (for recovery?)

If you organise your time effectively and carefully, you can fit a lot in. It's a matter of being creative with your time and remembering that you don't have to fit everything in from Monday to Friday. Some would argue that this sort of timetabling is too inflexible for university life – but it will help you find a balance and you can always change things around.

Getting things done

It can be a great morale booster to make a list of things you need to do, set your own deadlines for doing them and to tick them off as you go – beating your deadlines. You'll need to become well practised at managing your time and prioritising at work, so university offers you a great chance to develop your skills in managing yourself!

Tips for settling in:

- If you are feeling terribly nervous, remember that everyone is in the same boat; smile and you'll look confident, even if you aren't.
- It will take time to find your way around – make use of any guided tours or go out with your new friends and see what you can find.
- Try not to go home often in the first term – it will make it harder to settle.
- If you don't like discos and clubs (and there are lots of people who secretly don't) make use of coffee and tea gatherings; it is much easier to get to know people.
- Be honest about it if you are having problems settling in. Lots of other students will be feeling the same way!
- Don't sit in your room at night and mope. Get out and meet people: clubs, societies, local church – anything, even if it's not connected with the university.
- Watch your spending – don't blow your money in the first week.

There'll probably be some departmental events and you'll either hear of these via your pigeon hole in the department or pick up details when you register. It's a good chance to meet all your tutors and lecturers plus other students out of a classroom setting. There'll invariably be someone doing the same subject as you in your hall – go together.

In the first few weeks, you may find things particularly stressful or particularly enjoyable. Whichever:

- Get enough sleep.
- Don't miss lectures – they will help you get into a routine with all your new-found freedom.
- Get some exercise (usually taken care of by endless tours round buildings, libraries, etc).
- Watch your budget – remember that your grant has to last and your chances of winning the National Lottery are umpteen million to one.

- Plan your time carefully. ('I haven't made breakfast once this week – my first meal of the day is a Mars Bar and a coffee.')
- If you're having problems settling in, talk to someone, like a student counsellor.

Moving to a new lifestyle

The first two or three weeks can seem like a blast. You love the change of scene, you're enjoying meeting people, you may take your first weekend trip to a beautiful part of the country, and try new activities. And then, you find yourself getting tired of it. Your body and brain suddenly start saying, 'Well, it's been very nice, but it's time to go home now.' You've been at university for what seems like an extended holiday and your body is telling you that the vacation is over, it's time to get back to normality. You suddenly realise: 'Hey, I'm here for a long time' – a year or more. You may find yourself starting to yearn for home and be surprised – and a little angry that you're feeling let down about it. University was supposed to be fun, the best time ever. So what's going on?

Times like these do pass and help you to grow – you'll soon settle down again. Particularly for international students, national holidays such as Thanksgiving and Christmas can be hard if you're apart from your family. Get a short break away and travel to take your mind off it, to plan an event with your new-found British friends or to meet up with people from your home country to celebrate the holiday in style in Britain itself. The International Office or counselling services will listen and give advice.

'I like meeting people'

If you're one of these people who put this meaningless phrase on their CV, the good news is that you can certainly fulfil this interest at university. You'll come into contact with hundreds of people: your fellow students who may be aged from 18 to 80 plus from all over the world and professional people who look even more harassed than you do as they rush from work to lecture, mobile phone in hand.

Your daily life will now consist of meeting the finest brains in the country ('Now, what did I say we were going to discuss today?'), including lecturers, heads of department, professors, vice-chancellors, registrars, admissions tutors, deans, personal tutors, readers, research fellows and associates, directors – people dedicated to doing research, to teaching and to moving the university forward. Then there'll be the non-academics, many of them graduates in their own right, working in finance, buildings, resources, accommodation, personnel, the library and marketing. And there's the support staff who actually *run* the place – secretaries, librarians, technicians, clerical staff, administrative staff, porters, catering staff, wardens, counsellors, health officers; they are all concerned with the day-to-day organisation and running of the university. They will all enter into your lives and you'll learn from each and every one of them.

You'll meet employers, who may be brought in to lecture, assess, set projects, talk about their organisation and its career paths and to be persuaded to provide finance for the university. Employers will ask the university for help in training and educating their employees, plus research projects and expert advice and knowledge. And there'll inevitably be reps from the community, sitting on various bodies to ensure that the needs of the local community are met by the university where feasible

Where else would you meet such a diverse body of people? Make the most of it.

Make the most of chances to learn about the university's resources – it will save you stacks of time

Make sure you know what computing facilities are available, along with technical help. Many students bring their own computer or lap top to university with them – make sure it's insured. Most universities have invested heavily in IT facilities so make the most of them. Many also have access to JANET, the UK academic computer network.

These days, there are far more students after the library resources than there used to be. Many libraries have developed strategies for coping with their shortage of resources, such as systems for overnight loans, 24-hour loans, 4-hour loans and inter-library loans, but you may still find that resources are stretched to the limit. Take advantage of the resources/library/media tour at the start of term if there is one – it'll enable you to make the most of what is there.

Resource centres offer access to basic texts on the reading lists you were sent or given; background reading material, journals, slides, videos, cassettes, company reports, statistics and rare books. Libraries also offer photocopying facilities, quiet study areas, technical support and a help desk. There will also be media and computing centres for you to find your way around. Some departments will have established their own library in addition to the central one.

Some students have pulled together as a group and share library books between them; but this requires a strong spirit of cooperation and goodwill, good organisation and no 'hangers-on' down the line. Others have finely developed skills in hiding the vital reference book everyone wants so that *they* alone can access it.

Eating places

You can eat in a catering hall (even if you live out, you can in some cases buy a meal ticket for the term or an individual meal), at student bars, coffee shops, snack bars, cafeterias in university buildings, do take-aways, at pubs, inexpensive restaurants for a treat (they may offer discounts for students) or cook your own! Where there are students, cheap eating establishments will exist. Some students manage to live on £10 for food each week.

Coming out

For many gays, lesbians and bi-sexuals, university is a paradise because they can be open about their feelings for the first time in their lives. There's the sheer relief of talking about your sexuality without anyone judging you and there are usually gay, lesbian and bi-sexual clubs which organise loads of activities.

Sex

Yes, you can get pregnant the first time you have sex if you're not using contraceptives. If you're going to have sex, use contraceptives and use a condom to protect yourself against HIV. Visit the Health Centre at your Student Union for advice. Of course, you could always say no.

Drugs

Getting involved with drugs can have serious consequences for your future career, especially if you get caught. Many employers won't recruit people with a record or past involvement with drugs or even those who might be on drugs for a number of reasons. How do they know you're not still taking drugs? Might you use the firm for drugs purposes? Will they make your thinking foggy? Will they make you indiscreet? Drugs give you a high for a few hours but they could also land you with a record with all its inevitable consequences for far longer. Still, it's your life and your choice. You know what you're doing.

Student societies and clubs

There are loads of clubs and societies – the student parents' society, mature students' society, engineering, film, geography, gay, lesbian and bisexual, Christian union, law, swimming, skiing, circus skills, Afro-Caribbean, Malaysian, wine, Labour, Conservative, cricket... the list is endless. Societies give you a great way to make new friends and you can try something you've never tried before – parachuting? Hang-gliding? Getting into politics? The animal rights movement?

Many universities will also have societies that are related to courses, for example history, conservation and engineering societies. One advantage of joining these is that they can provide evidence of interest in and a passion for your subject (which employers will give you a plus for). Also, your involvement in them may assist you in developing transferable skills such as planning and organising. Some of the more vocational societies may involve employers coming to talk about career topics and could provide useful links for the future.

You might want to get involved with the local community through Community Action, doing voluntary projects like helping in homes for the elderly. Or work for the student magazine (helpful if you want to get into journalism, the media, PR) or be a member of the ENTS Committee, helping to organise entertainment like concerts, gigs, discos, etc. This could involve getting local bands or major groups.

If your university doesn't have a society to cater for your interests, you can always start one up.

> **'**A group of us discovered we were all Winnie the Pooh addicts and so we formed a Winnie the Pooh Appreciation Society. We used to take picnics on walks over the moors and pretend we were going to find the North Pole. We always found a pub instead of the North Pole, but we saw some fantastic scenery, enjoyed the walking – and had a lot of fun.**'**   Jane, history graduate, primary teacher

Some international students welcome the chance to meet up with fellow nationals through the network of clubs and societies; however, these should not be the only societies you should join, or you won't meet any British students.

The Student Union/Association/Guild

Get to know your way around the Union. It's *the* place to:

- grab a cheap coffee and sandwich
- enjoy a pint
- get a part-time job
- do laundry
- get general enquiries answered by helpful staff
- find out what's going on now and in the future
- get involved – most unions either employ or ask for volunteers to run it
- pick up the student magazine
- get medical advice, book a flight, cash a cheque, buy books, stationery, cigarettes
- not remember what you did on Friday night
- remember what you did on Saturday night and wish you hadn't
- meet people
- gossip one minute and debate world issues the next
- find people who'll understand your problem and try to help you sort it out
- go to concerts, discos, comedy nights, quiz evenings, union meetings...

You don't *have* to be a member to do any of these things because the 1994 Education Act gave you the right to opt out of Union membership. But you do need to be a member to vote in or stand at elections. Plus a Student Union Card will provide you with many discounts locally, nationally and internationally.

Your Union will work with the National Union of Students, which represents the interests of students throughout Britain, telling Parliament and the press what you think. It also gives training and back up to the elected officials at your local level. It should also be well represented on all the major decision-making and planning bodies at the university or college so that students' view can be taken into account. Why not put yourself forward as a rep?

Studying ('What?')

Remember, the student intake is different

For one thing, the emphasis of many courses in British education has changed lower down the ladder and universities are having to provide extra courses to make up the difference. People are entering university with a far wider spectrum of qualifications than they used to and there are more of them. Lecturers have had to alter first-year courses to suit and get everyone up to the same standard by the end of the first year.

Learning methods

Methods of learning are continually expanding and many institutions of higher education have won awards for their innovative techniques of teaching. There's more emphasis on learning by doing, so you may find yourself doing role play, video conferencing, projects, mock trials in law courses, and case studies – often live, suggested by employers. Language labs and lab practicals are important parts of the course for language and science students respectively, while arts students can expect a few lectures and seminars, backed up by their own extensive reading. Computer-based learning offers you the chance to become familiar with IT, but you'll still be writing dissertations (probably), essays and reports. Work placements are invaluable ways to learn about work and to apply your theoretical knowledge to the workplace. The 'chalk and talk' approach where the lecturer drones on for 50 minutes to a hall of yawning students is decreasing in importance, but make use of them. Many lecturers base the exam on their lectures. Make key notes with headings so that everything is clear, but don't expect to write them up 'in neat' afterwards – you'll be too busy racing to the library to get the books the tutor's recommended you read before everyone else gets there. Anyway, don't be afraid to try new learning methods – after all, you're at university to learn. It will teach you to handle the unexpected!

Arts and social science students get less formal teaching than science students – anything from eight to 12 hours a week, usually in a lecture, seminar and tutorial. The rest of the time, they are supposed to spend studying and reading on their own. You have to be very motivated and determined to study.

So test your motivation – which would you rather do:

► background reading for the seminar on women's writers in 20th century America/write up the day's practical (as you should)?
► meet friends off your course for a coffee or a/several pint/s in the Union?
► head off for a game of squash followed by a drink *(healthy)*?
► laundry (your socks are standing up on their own)?

Such are the choices you'll have to make. You can see why it's important to be a committed, motivated student.

Classes are much larger than they used to be and tutors have less time for individual meetings, so you must take responsibility for your own learning and have good self-management skills to succeed in higher education.

Books

You will probably get a list of suggested books to buy for the course. Don't. They are not all essential and after the first few weeks you'll get an idea of those that it's going to be extremely useful to have a copy of and those that you can take from the library. If you're really keen, buy second-hand if you can or form a small group with your new classmates and agree to buy one book each and lend them around – you'll need to be very cooperative if this approach is to work.

Working out how much to do

At a British university, it's up to you how much work you do and when you do it. No one will run after you shouting for essays or assignments. You may be given an essay to write, plus a deadline (a term away) and no one will mention it to you again, although tutors will obviously be willing to discuss suitable topics with you and try to help with any problems you have. It's up to you to remember you've got a deadline to meet.

You get out of higher education as much as you're prepared to put in

Much will depend on how far you really prepare yourself for sessions with your tutor. If you did no background reading because you chose to go out drinking with your new friends instead four or five times a week, the chances are you'll blow your grant and sit in the seminar like a dumb lemon, listening to what everyone else is saying, giving the occasional intellectual nod and sliding down in your chair praying the lecturer won't ask you what you think. You can only get out of a higher education course as much as you put in. It's all a question of balance.

Preparing for the seminar

You'll be given a list of suggested reading. It's up to you how much you read of it. But you'll also be expected to find some reading of your own to do outside of the list. You'll be asked to lead seminars, perhaps with a paper you've prepared earlier.

> 'Now, next week, what would you like to discuss? The rise of the medieval monasteries. Right. I'd like someone to prepare a ten minute talk on the reasons for the rise. Any volunteers? John, what about you? Thank you. Just ten minutes, then, on what you think caused the rise and then we'll open it up for discussion. I'll see you all next week.'
> History lecturer

Prepare your paper with an introduction, followed by your discussion/argument/facts and conclusion. Don't read it out in a monotone. Use index cards and talk to your audience – a daunting but excellent preparation for work.

For some, the first year may be easy

When you take into account the range of qualifications you can now enter many higher education courses with, both British and international, you'll see why some courses have altered their first year's course content. You may find you're repeating stuff you did in further education, but it's only because lecturers have to make sure that everyone reaches the end of the year with the right amount of knowledge. Some universities are running classes like remedial grammar in language classes or elementary mathematics.

'I've chosen the wrong course! I want to swap!'

Check out what options there are and discuss them with your personal tutor, and a careers counsellor if you wish. Students do change courses, although the likelihood will depend on your entry requirements and how flexible the institution is. You must tell your LEA in writing *before* you make the commitment to change course or to withdraw. You can withdraw from a course for up to 20 weeks without losing your entitlement for a full award for another course.

And there'll always be friendly rivalry between courses. Who does the most work?

The alternative prospectus from the University of Sheffield displays well the friendly rivalry between the various faculties.

Q. Why don't arts students look out of the window in the mornings?
A. It gives them nothing to do in the afternoons.

Get ready to justify all that hard work you have to do.

Rag week

British students are a generous bunch, even though they are penniless themselves. Rag raised £2.5 million for various charities in 1996 and students had a great time into the bargain, doing wild, wacky and occasionally illegal things. Hit squads masked with balaclavas and armed with custard do a pretty good job. Book one for a friend in lectures.

Parents

In all the excitement of your new life, *don't* forget your parents. They have given you much support in your efforts to reach university. Send them postcards, just to say, 'Thinking of your cooking, mum,' or, 'Thinking of you.' Because, believe it or not, it's hard for parents when their 'children' move away from home – it's a sign that *they* are getting older. So remember them, and not just when you need to make the phone call beginning, 'Mum, you know you sent me that cheque – thank you very much – umm – err – I'm afraid I've spent it all. Books, you know.'

Going home for the holidays

When you get home from your first time away, things will be different. You may need to re-establish some ground rules about going out at night. Everyone at home has got on with their lives and made lots of decisions while you were away that may come as a surprise. Allow for lots of give and take on both sides. Use the opportunity to meet up with old friends, pop in to school and tell them how you're getting on.

Back again for a new term

January... sick and tired of January

Back in January, you may have the January blues. Lots of people suffer these. There isn't the same excitement as there was at the start of the autumn term; the weather is awful, most people are *really* broke after Christmas and worse still, there's lots of work to be done and exams to face. Throw a party, get away for a day, do something wild and wacky. It will soon pass.

'HELP!!! I can't stand it anymore'

If things just aren't going well and you can't figure out why, don't worry but do take action. There are masses of people around who'll try to help you:

- ► Counselling services, often run by the Student Union, such as Nightline (student volunteers) or those employed by the university in the health centre.
- ► Health services – there to listen and advise on dealing with stress.
- ► Finance office – sort financial problems out before they grow.
- ► Tutors – yes, they are very busy but they are there to help. Ask them in advance for a time you can go and talk to them.
- ► Student Union – they'll understand and reassure you and give advice on a wide range of matters.
- ► Student advisers in banks – again, they'll help you sort out a solution.
- ► International office – if you're feeling homesick, fed up of feeling as if you're in Antarctica, and can't understand anything you're

going through, go and visit this office. They will reassure you that what you're experiencing is quite normal and that the average Brit is fed up with the weather as well.

- ► Chaplain – the Church will listen and give practical, helpful advice.
- ► Disabled adviser – can help you solve any problems.
- ► Friends – many of them may be feeling the same way.

'How can we influence the direction of the university as students?'

British students are certainly becoming more vocal about their discontent, encouraged by the Charter of Higher Education and the fact that many of them are contributing towards at least their living expenses. Universities have Student Charters, put together in consultation with students and academic staff, stating their responsibilities – and yours. Students should be represented throughout the university at every level through a system of course reps, places on committees and boards, questionnaires and surveys.

Institutions differ in their involvement of students in academic course planning, university business plans and departmental matters, but they are certainly more accountable than they used to be. You can also get a copy of the Charter for Higher Education from your local (careers) library or the Department for Education and Employment.

'I've got a complaint'

If you're having problems, for example with harassment or discrimination, talk to your Union, but take notes of the difficulties you're experiencing as you go so that you can build up evidence of specific things that have upset you or caused you concern. Counsellors may be able to suggest ways to deal with the problem without taking official action. For example, if you're unhappy with your tutor, keep a record of the reasons why, eg, 'He was late', 'He didn't turn up' or, 'He never marks our work.' Enlist the support of other students and make your complaint before the exams or any assessments are done.

If you've got a partner, work together

People do change as their horizons widen and they discover new knowledge, develop different skills and meet people on their course.

Partners should work to keep the avenues of communication open, find time to do activities you both enjoy together and it may be helpful if the partner not involved in studying can find something new to do so that they also grow and develop.

Second year considerations. 'Wait a minute. What if I fail the first year?'

One student commented recently that universities don't like failing people because it doesn't make them look good. Seriously, if you're worried you're not going to do well, talk to your tutor as problems start arising, not when you're knee-deep in them. If you're ill, get a medical certificate. Sit the exams whatever, because if you don't, you'll lose your contribution to a grant. Normally, if you have exams to resit, you'll do that at the end of the summer. This means that you have to spend your summer revising, so get them first time round if you can.

'Where am I going to live next?'

The first year passes very quickly and in the land of luxury in a hall of residence or self-catering unit. Your heating, lighting and water is catered for. *In February*, start thinking about where you are going to live in the second year – and more importantly, *who* you want to live with. Living with other people can really test friendships. There's always one person who doesn't pull their weight with the bills and think it's all right to be behind with the rent and won't clean the loo when it's their turn. Rotate among you those boring responsibilities like cleaning, buying food and cooking. Work out what bills need to be covered and how you are going to cover them early on – it will save a lot of arguing. Throw a house-warming party, decide who is going to provide what ('Do we really need two CD players?') and check all your stuff is insured.

The good accommodation vanishes like magic, so start your search early and seek advice from third-year students: they will be able to tell you who the good landlords are ('We had a problem with the drain in the kitchen and they sorted it out the same day') and which ones to avoid: 'Charges the earth, expects you to share with bugs of all sorts and never fixed the problem with the lighting the whole time we were there.' Anyway, most third-years are leaving so they won't want their accommodation. Get information and advice from your accommodation office too and if you try a housing agency, make sure it is a reputable one.

If you are going to rent private accommodation:

- *don't* check it out alone, for your own personal safety
- get a written lease with a copy of the Rent Book
- get someone else to check the lease before you sign it
- sort out who is paying for what and that it is all serviced regularly (eg, water, gas, electricity) – check this is clear with your landlord and your flatmates
- get an inventory of all the furnishings provided, if any
- check whether insurance companies will ensure goods in the area – it may be a 'no go' area because of high crime rates
- know what you need to provide in the way of utensils, linen, etc.

Tip for parents: some parents buy a house as an investment for their offspring to use, and rent the other rooms out to fellow students. Talk to your bank manager if this appeals and remember that the house may not look pretty when you visit, whatever it looked like when you first saw it.

Planning your second year

You may have many decisions to make as you approach the end of your first year regarding the options you plan to take next. Read any litera-ture given to you carefully so that you understand the implications of your choice; talk to second- and third-years about the different options, how the work load differs, and get their advice.

Make good use of those vacations

The entire length of your course, holidays included, should enable you to add a great deal of valuable currency to your CV. You'll probably get work to do from university, but it's a useful chance to work in new surroundings too.

'I worked in the holidays, temping for local businesses. This developed my ability to cope with changing circumstances, to form working relationships with others quickly, to adjust to new ways of doing things and it increased my business awareness. It also helped

me extend the network of contacts I was trying to develop for the future. It also helped considerably with my finances. '
                    Janie, business studies student, spent summers temping

Even if you've got holiday reading to do, try to fit it in with something else. This especially goes for the long summer holidays when you could get some work experience, do paid work, travel, get a driving licence, pick up a language. Employers will want to see how you've spent your free time – it gives them a clue about how motivated you are to *do* things. Make use of your Student Union card and all the deals it gives you with the ISIC card (International Student Identity Card).

'Help. I'm about to go on work experience'

Work experience placements enable you to network with people at work, develop your transferable skills and give you a chance to apply specialist knowledge to the workplace. You could end up with a job offer, they may help financially; you can do work experience abroad thus enhancing your career prospects.

More points to check:

- Has the company you're assigned to got a clear idea of what work experience is about?
- How is your placement monitored by the university?
- How often do your tutors visit?
- Who can you get help from if things aren't going well?
- Do you have a clear picture of what you are expected to achieve in your placement, from the employers' view point, your tutors' and your own?

Get stuck in and enjoy your year. Remember to give yourself extra time to get there on your first day, to join in everything you can – and to give a lot back.
    Finally, a piece of advice from a typical graduate:

'Make the most of every day you've got. It all goes far too quickly. '
                    Kate, urban planner, working for a local authority

SUMMARY EXERCISES

- ▶ Don't forget that if things are going wrong, there are plenty of people around who will want to help – even if they are pushed for time.
- ▶ Make the most of every day of your time as a university student – not just in term time but in the holidays too.
- ▶ It's a chance to try out new interests as well as continue old ones. Dare yourself to do something different every term, even if it's a one-off.
- ▶ What do you want to do during your time at university? Make up a list and compare notes with a couple of friends to bounce ideas off each other.
- ▶ What do you want to achieve through your higher education years? What do you think an employer wants you to achieve? Why?
- ▶ Visit the library to check out activities you can get involved in during the holidays.

TEN

Thinking ahead. ('What, again?')

Time passes quickly when you're having fun

'But I've only just *started* my degree. Can't I have a rest from careers?'

University days sneak past very quickly and usually without your noticing. Before you know it, you're looking for second-year accommodation and deciding which friends to share with, then you're deciding what to do for your final year topics. And everyone back home is asking you, 'So, where's all this studying leading to, then?'

Many people start university courses with little idea of what they want to do at the end of them, so it's important to make use of university careers services early on. Even if you get a lower level job than you'd hoped for, these days a job is very much what you make of it. The more responsibility you take on, the more likely you are to create your own niche – and get the rewards to match.

Get to know your University Careers Service early on in your course

Some careers services will introduce themselves and what they can offer to you in a lecture. If they don't, find out where the service is and how it can help you. Most services will:

- have counsellors who will talk to you about your interests, values, needs and strengths and help you match those to jobs; advise you on application procedures, point out avenues of information
- have computer-aided guidance programmes
- have details of vacancies, not just long-term for graduates but also opportunities for summer and short-term work

► have a network of employers and past graduates who may be able to assist you in ascertaining your future direction – these people may be pulled in to assist with a careers education programme, eg, a talk on 'Interview technique' or 'The application process'.

What could you do after graduation?

► A postgraduate course which gives you vocational skills relevant to a particular career, such as heritage management, hospitality management.
► Do a postgraduate course involving research, with possibly some lecturing to pay your way through.
► A graduate training scheme with a company, for example in retail, management consultancy, computer consultancy, banking, finance, accountancy, law, training, recruitment agency.
► Find a 'graduate required' position where you work out your own training needs in consultation with the firm.
► Take time out – do something constructive for a year, like travel after working for six months to pay off the overdraft.
► Join a small firm with your vocational skills in a post that doesn't specify a degree but none the less requires specific competencies.

Finding a job during the holidays and after graduation

Many vacancies are not filled through advertising; if a company knows of someone who has the skills, abilities and attitude they are looking for, they will recruit them directly because it saves the company time. Small and medium sized companies form an important part of Britain's economy so they are worth investigating, especially if you have specific skills to offer. You may find that you need to start off on contract work, for example for a firm that is particularly busy with an extra workload. Watch the papers in the geographic areas you want to work in; firms who are expanding or who have just won a major contract may well need extra staff. Check *Kompass* in the public library for names and addresses of firms in the career area you want to work in.

Marketing yourself

- Take time over correspondence with employers.
- Get a reputation as someone who likes to put forward well thought out ideas and solutions.
- Do your research before you apply for a position – it shows seriousness and intent.

Get work experience in your career area of interest

Employers regard work experience with increasing importance. It is evidence that you have motivation, sure, but it also means that you'll be able to adapt that more quickly to the workplace and contribute to it. For many, it also provides them with evidence of your interest in and commitment to your career. For you, it provides a useful insight into different careers and organisations and will help you decide what sort of career you want – and what you're seeking in a future employer. So get work experience, even if it's unpaid.

Knowing how to find work at any stage of your degree

Make sure you are aware of all the different ways of getting a job, including:

- looking for job vacancies in the press, job centres, TECs, and careers services
- asking employers directly if they can make use of your skills by writing a letter with your CV enclosed
- signing up with a recruitment agency for temporary work – this often leads to a permanent job
- signing up with a recruitment agency to look for permanent work – have a good idea of what you want to do and what you can *offer* before you go
- surfing the Internet recruitment sites
- surfing recruitment agencies' vacancies on the Internet
- registering with PeopleBank the Employment Network; employers looking for recruits for short- and long-term work can check out your abilities and skills and if they like the look of you, request contact with you through PeopleBank
- networking

- starting up your own business after university
- becoming involved in network marketing
- buying a franchise operation (can be expensive)
- looking for work abroad.

The more proactive you are in your search for a job, the more likely it is to be the right one for you. You also need to be committed in terms of making an effort to go to the Careers Service (ie, finding the time to get there).

Start networking as early as you can in your course

Even if you are not sure what you want to do, get work experience which gives you an insight into business life. Make contacts, keep them and nurture them.

Excel at anything you do with any company, even if you are 'only with them for work experience'. If you are good, people will be happy to recommend you to others who are recruiting or the company may offer you a job when you graduate.

Don't forget that everyone at management level in a company has their own extensive network of contacts in all sorts of organisations. Show what you can do, use your initiative and come up with creative suggestions, and you will get noticed. You could always ask a manager for advice or help – most are happy to give it.

Profile your skills regularly

Track all those things you are:

- achieving
- learning
- doing
- contributing to.

Analyse them for skills, strengths and interests you are developing. You should be looking at profiling everything you do:

- in your course
- in extracurricular activities
- work experience, paid or unpaid, full-time or part-time
- voluntarily.

Track your achievements and activities throughout your degree and you'll be better able to identify those skills and interests you want to use at work, and to sell yourself to future employers. Employers don't want to waste resources in training someone who is clearly unmotivated and not going to succeed.

Getting your results

What results? At present, the grading for degrees runs like this:

1st	First	First
2:1	Upper Second	Two one
2:2	Lower Second	Two two
3rd	Third class	Third
Pass	Pass	Pass

There are calls to change this system, because more students are getting 2:1s and there is a debate over whether students are working harder and getting better results, or whether the standards are going down. It's harder for employers to determine those students who are in the upper part of the 2:1 band.

SUMMARY EXERCISES

▶ Investigate your options by making good use of the careers service.
▶ Don't leave it until the final year – you won't be able to think as clearly when you're burdened down with final year work.
▶ Keep a record of your activities to show that you are an achiever who likes to get results.
▶ Make the most of the best years of your life!
▶ What would you like to achieve during your holidays at university? Put some ideas down on paper.
▶ What goals do you want to achieve in the next year? The next five years? And the next ten?
▶ What excites you most about the future?

Your energy, your motivation
Your life, your choice
Good luck!

Glossary

Academic Board Deals with all academic matters and advises the
Principal and Board of Governors accordingly, working
through small committees.

Accelerated degree courses Doing a three-year degree programme
in two years – some places give you the chance to do this,
especially in the more vocational areas. Mature students like
them in particular.

Access course A fast track qualification for mature students seeking
to enter higher education.

ACIB The professional qualification for staff employed in the
banking industry. A successful student is an Associate of the
Chartered Institute of Bankers.

Admissions tutor Has responsibility for admissions to the
department and may therefore make the decision about
your application.

Affiliated courses Those courses validated by traditional universities.

AGCAS The Association of Graduate and Careers Advisory
Services.

Alumni association Most universities have one, consisting of
former students of the institution.

APL The Accreditation of Prior Learning (more applicable to
mature students). Any relevant work experience or
qualifications may be accredited or counted towards the
course you're applying to.

Applied course One where the knowledge is applied to
engineering, business, technology.

ARELS Association of Recognised English Language Services. It
provides a list of British Council recognised English
language schools.

Armed Forces units Attached to many higher education
institutions – check the prospectus for further details.

Associate colleges These work with a university in the
development of their higher education provision. They are a

full partner in the planning and funding process for the development of partnership provision.

Associate Student Scheme   You can try out a subject by taking one or two modules or units.

Award   Another name for 'qualification' but also covers the term 'financial awards' or grants made by local educational authorities, usually covering tuition fees plus a contribution towards living expenses.

Board of Governors   The supreme body in new universities which meets termly to determine the way forward and which involves members from the local community, leaders in industry, etc.

BA   Bachelor of Arts – the qualification awarded to a degree covering arts, humanities, plus possibly social science, business and management studies depending on the slant of the course.

BEd   Bachelor of Education – the qualification name given to a degree covering the study of education. These degrees are aimed at those wishing to become (primary) teachers.

BEng   Bachelor of Engineering – a name given to a degree covering engineering subjects.

BMusic   Bachelor of Music.

BSc   Bachelor of Science – this qualification will cover the sciences including biology, chemistry, physics, psychology and mathematics plus technical subjects such as computer science.

BTEC   Business and Technician Education Council.

Bursar   The person in charge of money – the chief finance officer.

BUSA   British Universities Sporting Association.

Career Development Loans   Loans available for people in Britain who wish to train for a vocational qualification lasting less than two years.

CATS   Credit Accumulation and Transfer Scheme which enables you to transfer credit between institutions.

CDL   Career Development Loan. A loan to support a vocational course.

Certificate of Higher Education/CertHE   A qualification awarded for the successful completion of a course equivalent to the first year of a degree course.

Chancellor The head of a university, often a public figure or even a member of the Royal Family, usually a ceremonial post.
Combined award This qualification covers a course where several subjects are studied, eg, English, history and French. Combined honours may be named as such where insufficient emphasis on one subject has warranted a subject name in the award title (eg, 75 per cent English, 25 per cent history, French and economics).
Core The essential, necessary bits to study within a degree programme. You may have to study them in a certain order.
Council The chief executive and financial body, responsible for the university's relationship with external agencies. Usually includes people from the local community and public life.
Court The top body in a traditional university chaired by the chancellor and with wide representation on it including people from the TUC, CBI and learned societies.
CRAC Careers Research Advisory Centre. Seeks to help people make wise career decisions and is an independent national organisation which promotes sound careers guidance. It runs courses and conferences and produces literature plus publications via Biblios PDS Ltd, Star Road, Partridge Green, West Sussex RH13 9LD.
Credits Each module or course may have a specific number of credits, which will vary from one institution to another depending on the organisation of the scheme.
CSV Community Service Volunteers – a voluntary scheme lasting four to 12 months in which you volunteer to commit yourself to the community and help improve the quality of other people's lives.
CVCP The Committee of Vice Chancellors and Principals, an influential body.

Day release A course where the student is released by his employer from the workplace to attend a course at a higher education institution.
Dean The head of a faculty.
Department Most institutions are divided into faculties or schools, then again into departments.
Departmental Academic Board This advises the head of department on the academic programme, course regulations, allocates duties between staff, etc. It discusses student welfare and progress.

Diploma of Higher Education/DipHE   This award is given for the successful completion of a course equivalent to the first two years of a full-time degree course.

These courses tend to be more general in nature than degrees and usually two A-levels or equivalent are required. A useful course, especially for mature students who only want to do two years. Check before you start, however, to see if you can continue on to the final year of a degree course after successful completion of a Diploma in Higher Education.

Direct entry   Advanced entry to a course at a stage after year one. Also known as advanced standing.

Director   The chief academic and administrator in the new universities.

Distance learning   Courses with an institution where you study at home.

ECCTIS   ECCTIS 2000 is the organisation that runs ECCTIS, a computerised information system normally available at careers services and schools.

Education system (British)   Involves in order of progression: primary (5–11 years), secondary (11–16), both compulsory, and further (16+) and higher education (usually 17/18+). Preparation in further education is usually essential to enter higher education.

EEA   European Economic Area.

EHE   Enterprise in Higher Education, a scheme designed to strengthen students skills for the workplace.

Elective   A term used to describe a module the student can choose or elect to do – it's not compulsory as the **core** subject is. Thus a medical student could choose an elective in a management subject.

ENTS   The committee or group of students responsible for putting together the entertainment programme, eg, clubs, discos, concerts, bands, gigs.

ERASMUS   European Union Action Scheme for Mobility of University Students (or, more simply – a study exchange programme within the European Union).

Eurling   European Engineer, the European equivalent of Chartered Engineer.

Extended degrees   Extended degree programmes include an introductory year for those with inappropriate entry qualifications at advanced level. The year forms an integral part of a degree course.

Faculty   The administrative centre of academic staff, led by a dean with the help of lecturing and administrative staff.

Faculty Board   Tends to make decisions on university policy concerning an area of study, eg, English and American studies; engineering.

Fees   The money paid to the higher education institution for tuition. These vary according to your subject and status, ie, home or overseas.

Foundation course   A full-time course available in certain subjects for students with inappropriate or insufficient academic qualifications or for people who've changed their minds about their career direction since enrolling in further education; also known as Year Zero or Extended Degrees. Check grant implications if you want to sign up for them.

GATE Project   A project which has been working to support GNVQ students who are applying to higher education. Part of its work includes developing selectors' understanding of the GNVQ.

GCSE   General Certificate of Secondary Education, equivalent to the old O-level; these exams are taken by most students at the end of compulsory secondary education in Britain.

Going rate   The level of entry qualifications which are expected – although they'll change from one year to the next.

Graduate   Someone who has successfully finished a degree – you in a few years' time!

HEFCE   Higher Education Funding Council for England, which seeks to promote high quality, cost-effective teaching and research within British higher education.

HELOA   Higher Education Liaison Officers Association – a group that has an expertise knowledge of higher education and which can advise you accordingly.

Heist   Heist is a self-funding company which does project work for individual higher education institutions; publishes policy research on education issues to British institutions; and organises conferences. It distributes prospectuses to schools, colleges and careers services throughout the UK and further afield. It also undertakes research and produces reports into higher education.

HEQC Higher Education Quality Council, which seeks to contribute to the improvement of quality in higher education institutions.

HNC Higher National Certificate, usually vocational courses studied on a part-time day-release basis. The equivalent of a first year of a full-time degree course.

HND Higher National Diploma: a wide range of vocational courses which are work-related and teach you relevant skills, competencies and knowledge so that you can hit the ground running when you start work. They are useful for entry to supervisory and technical-level work, or alternatively, they can provide a path to a related degree course. In some cases you can enter the second year of a degree course directly – you need to discuss your options with the appropriate admissions tutor. These full-time courses are used by many students as a stepping stone from further education courses such as A-levels or GNVQs. HND/C to degree level entry are recognised by professional bodies, and may lead to exemptions from professional examinations if the course content is appropriate. Some courses offer you sandwich placements.

(Hons) A degree with honours has a higher value than one without, because the 'honours' bit provides the grades or classification of your degree, ie, first (1), upper second (2:1), lower second (2:2) or third (3). A degree without honours or classification is called a pass degree or an **ordinary degree**.

IELTS International English Language Testing Service – a popular entrance test for overseas students seeking to enter higher education in Britain.

ILC Irish Leaving Certificate.

Interdiscplinary course Enables you to study a range of subjects across several disciplines.

JANET The Joint Academic Network which provides access to electronic mailboxes and specialist facilities in other UK universities and throughout the world.

Joint honours The study of two subjects at degree level – you get a degree in, for example, philosophy and mathematics, having studied them on an equal weighting.

LEA   Local Education Authority.

Lecturer   The person who lectures, teaches, researches and publishes. If they are teaching on vocational courses, they should have worked in industry.

Lecturer, senior   A lecturer who's got over ten years' experience, usually with a good research record and teaching reports.

Licensed colleges   These do not have an exclusive arrangement with the university and deliver university courses at a foundation and first year level. Students have the same rights as those studying at the university.

LLB   Bachelor of Laws.

MA   Master of Arts: postgraduate study and award of arts or humanities subjects.

Major/Minor   A course where the student studies two subjects, with more emphasis on one than the other, eg, 65 per cent mathematics, 35 per cent physics, 75 per cent French, 25 per cent business studies. These become known as BSc (Hons) mathematics with physics, or BA (Hons) French with business studies.

Mature student   The term for students normally over the age of 21, but 23 or 25 in a few institutions.

MBA   Master of Business Administration: postgraduate study and award of business – many degrees require that students have a couple of years' work experience prior to starting the course.

MEng   Master of Engineering – an undergraduate degree with extended and enhanced study of engineering.

MLitt   Master of Literature – a postgraduate award.

MPharm   Master of Pharmacy – a postgraduate award.

MPhil   Master of Philosophy – a postgraduate award.

MSc   Master of Science – postgraduate award and study of the sciences.

NVQs   National Vocational Qualifications; work-related and assessed courses.

Option   Like the elective, this is an optional element – you can choose from a range of options in a specific subject. Those available may depend on the staff's research interests and strong links with other departments.

Ordinary degree   An award without classification or final grading.
Organ award   Made by various colleges at Oxford and Cambridge
    to a successful candidate applying to help with or take
    charge of the music in the college chapel and to take an
    active part in the musical activities of the college in general.
    Some colleges state a preference or require candidates to
    read for Honours in the school of music. Contact the colleges
    themselves for further details.
Oxbridge   Oxford and Cambridge.

Personal tutor   Most higher education institutions allocate students
    a personal tutor, designed to assist with any personal
    problems you're having.
PGCE   Postgraduate Certificate of Education – a teacher training
    course for graduates lasting one year.
PgD   Postgraduate Diploma.
PhD   Doctor of Philosophy.
Placement   Period of time spent by the student gaining work
    experience in industry, paid or unpaid.
Postgraduate   The student who has done a first degree but is doing
    further study or research. The term 'postgraduate' is also
    used to describe a qualification – an MSc is a postgraduate
    award. These courses may be research oriented or
    instruction based, and many part-time vocational and/or
    professional courses are available, frequently for professionals
    working in the field and validated by professional bodies.
    Many graduates follow postgraduate vocational courses to
    prepare themselves for an area of employment.
Principal   In England and Wales, the Principal or Director is the
    chief academic and administrative executive in the newer
    universities and may be assisted by an Academic Director.
Pure courses   These are theoretical and academic in nature.

Reader   A senior lecturer who has an excellent record in research
    and publication.
Rector   The Chair in some Scottish universities; generally a public
    figure from the world of affairs or show business.
Registrar   The chief administrator in relation to academic matters
    who advises on and implements policy.
Research associate   A junior member of staff usually helping a
    more senior member on research.

Research fellow   Senior member of staff who works on research independently and may supervise other research workers. They may be financed from outside the university, eg, by organisations which want research done in a given area.

Sandwich   Course spent with one year or less acquiring work experience in industry as an integral part of the course – a chance to put theory into practice! Most sandwich courses last for four years, the third year being spent in industry.

SCE   Scottish Certificate of Education.

SCOTCAT   Scottish Credit Accumulation and Transfer Scheme.

SCOTVEC   Scottish Vocational Education Council.

Semester   Most higher education institutions now divide the academic year into two semesters: either September to December and January to May, or late September/early October to mid-January, late January to mid-June.

Senate   A body in the more traditional universities which deals with major issues and which manages much of its work through smaller committees which report and advise accordingly.

Single honours   The name given to an honours award with one named subject, eg, BA (Hons) German.

SOCRATES   This programme is designed to promote student mobility throughout Europe and it incorporates **ERASMUS** (study abroad) and LEONARDO (work experience) and TEMPUS (Central and East European exchanges).

Starting dates   Most courses start in late September/early October, but you can now start some programmes in January or February depending on the institution. Check with individual prospectuses. Part-time and modular degrees offer more flexibility.

Subject to approval   This phrase in a prospectus indicates that the course was being planned when the prospectus was being produced. Courses must undergo examination before being approved.

SVQs   Scottish Vocational Qualifications. The Scottish equivalent to GNVQs and NVQs in England, Wales and Ireland.

SWAS   Social Work Admissions System.

Terms   The traditional university year consists of three terms: late September/early October to early/mid-December, early January to mid-March and late April to the end of June.

Although many institutions still work on three terms, they have laid a two-semester system on top.

TOEFL Test of English as a Foreign Language.

UCAS University and Colleges Admissions System.

Unclassified degree A degree without Honours classification.

Undergraduate A student studying for a degree.

Unit A discrete element of a course. Successful completion leads to the award of credit.

Vice Chancellor The Chief Executive. May be called the Principal in Scotland.

Year in Industry A scheme enabling you to acquire relevant work experience in a real job with pay between school and university. You'll get key skills training plus the possibility of sponsorship in a field related to your degree.

Further information

Essentials

The University and College Entrance the Official Guide (annual) published by the Universities and Colleges Admissions System (UCAS) at Fulton House, Jessop Avenue, Cheltenham, Gloucestershire GL50 3SH.

The UCAS Handbook (annual), obtainable from UCAS, Fulton House, Jessop Avenue, Cheltenham, Gloucestershire GL50 3SH, or schools, colleges and careers offices. The handbook lists in alphabetical order the universities and colleges which admit students through UCAS and the subjects available.

Students' Guide to Higher Education (Colleges and Institutes of Higher Education), published free by the Standing Conference of Principals. Obtainable from Mr G R Mann, Administrative Officer, Standing Conference of Principals, Edge Hill College of Higher Education, Ormskirk, Lancashire L39 4QP.

COSHEP/UCAS Entrance Guide to Higher Education in Scotland (annual) published by the Committee of Scottish Higher Education Principals, St Andrew House, 141 West Nile Street, Glasgow G1 2RN.

Directory of Higher Education and *Directory of Further Education,* Hobsons Publishing .

Survey of HND Courses, by Eric Whittington, published by Trotman & Co.

GNVQs and Higher Education, 1997: Opportunities for GNVQ applicants, published by and available from UCAS.

The nitty gritty

The Potter Guide to Higher Education (annual) by S Potter and P Clarke, published by Dalebank Books. Information about higher education institutions and their environment. Also available on CD-ROM.

CRAC Degree Course Guide series, published by Hobsons Publishing. Comparative first degree course guides titled by degree subject, all of which are updated every two years. Prospectuses, produced by institutions to give further detail on the subjects they offer, their location, facilities, etc. Available in schools, colleges, careers offices, some libraries and individual institutions if you request direct help. Not available from UCAS.

How to Complete your UCAS Form, by Tony Higgins, published by Trotman and Co. Trotman also produces a series of *Getting into* books which give specialist advice on how to make a successful application.

Going to University, by John McIlroy and Bill Jones, published by Manchester University Press, 1993. Lots of invaluable information about how the higher education system works, applying, finance and studying successfully.

Mature Students Handbook, by I Rosier and L Earnshaw, published by Trotman and Co. Surveys courses and career opportunities.

The Parents Guide to Higher Education, published and available free of charge from UCAS.

The PUSH Guide to Which University (annual) published by McGraw-Hill. Lots of useful information about specific universities and costs too! There is also a CD-ROM.

Careers related books

Occupations (annual) available from Careers and Information Centre (COIC), PO Box 298a, Thames Ditton, Surrey KT17 025; Tel: 0181 957 5030.

Careers with an Arts Degree, published by Hobsons Publishing.

Careers with a Science Degree, published by Hobsons Publishing.

What Do Graduates Do? The Association of Graduate and Careers Advisory Services. (Annual) published by Hobsons Publishing for Careers Research Advisory Centre (CRAC) Sheraton House, Castle Park, Cambridge CB3 0AC; Tel: 01223 460277.

Graduate Employment and Training (annual) published by Hobsons Publishing. Details thousands of prime graduate careers plus useful advice about what to do after your degree. On the Internet: http://www.get.co.uk

The HATFHE Handbook: The Handbook of Initial Teacher Training, listing courses of education for intending teachers. You can get a copy from Linneys ESL, 121 Newgate Lane, Mansfield, Nottinghamshire GH18 2PA.

Help with money

Career Development Loans. Call 0800 585 505 for a free booklet.

The Directory of Grant Making Trusts, published by Macmillan - unless you're in Scotland, in which case try the Scottish Education Department for information about the Register of Local Endowments.

Students Grants and Loans: A Brief Guide for Higher Education (annual). Obtainable free from the Department for Education and Employment Publications Centre, PO Box 2193, London E15 2EU. Available also from schools, colleges and careers services and some public libraries.

Guide to Students' Allowances, available free from the Scottish Education Department, Awards Branch, Gyleview, 3 Redheughs Riggs, South Gyle, Edinburgh EH12 9AH.

Awards and Loans to Students, available free from your local Education and Library Board or from the Department for Education and Employment, Scholarships Branch, Rathgael House, Balloo Road, Bangor, Co Down BT19 2PR.

Pay Your Way as a Student, by Alan Jamieson, CRAC Student Helpbooks, published by Hobsons Publishing. Lots of useful tips, including a savings plan for parents, a students' guide as to what the banks have to offer and information on postgraduate awards.

The Student Loan Scheme, Student Loan Company Limited, 100 Bothwell Street, Glasgow G2 7JD.

Sponsorships

The Sponsorship Year Book and *Sponsorship Insights*, available from Hollis Directories Ltd, Contact House, Lower Hampton Road, Sunbury, Middlesex TW16 5HQ.

The Which? Guide to Sponsorship in Higher Education, by Alan Jamieson, published by the Consumers Association and Hodder and Stoughton in association with Hobsons Publishing.

Engineering Opportunities for Students and Graduates (annual). Published by the Institution of Mechanical Engineers, Northgate Avenue, Bury St Edmunds, Suffolk IP32 6BN.

Give me a break! Take five!

A Year Off… A Year On? Suggestions for filling the gap! CRAC, Hobsons Publishing.

The Year in Industry, University of Manchester, Simon Building, Oxford Road, Manchester M13 9PL or e-mail khutchinson@fs3.eng.man.ac.uk

GAP Activity Projects, published by GAP Activity Projects (GAP) Ltd, GAP House, 44 Queen's Road, Reading, Berkshire RG1 4BB.

Gap Year Guidebook, published by Peridot Press, 2 Blenheim Crescent, London W11 1NN.

Study abroad

Studying in Europe, CRAC, Hobsons Publishing. Advice on where to go and how to get ready for this experience.

Directory of Jobs and Careers Abroad, Vacation Work, 9 Park End Street, Oxford OX1 1HJ.

The Central Bureau for Educational Visits and Exchanges, Seymour Mews House, Seymour Mews, London EC1H 9PE. Publishes several books on these areas, including *Volunteer Work Abroad, Working Holidays, A Year Between, Study Holidays*.

The European Education Yearbook: The annual guide to study abroad, published by Nexus Media.

Commonwealth Universities Yearbook, published by the Association of Commonwealth Universities, London.

Help for students with disabilities

Higher Education and Disability: A Guide to Higher Education for People with Disabilities (annual) published by Hobsons Publishing.

Financial Assistance for Students with Disabilities in Higher Education, available from SKILL, National Bureau for Students with Disabilities.

Help for mature students

How to Win as a Mature Student, Teresa Rickards, published by Kogan Page. This book will help you return to study after a break.

Help for overseas students

British University and College Courses, Trotman and Co.

International Qualifications for Entry to Higher Education, published by UCAS.

Overseas Students Offices:

Cyprus: Cultural Counsellor, Cyprus High Commission, 93 Park Street, London W1Y 4ET.

Guyana: The Education Attaché, Guyana High Commission, 3 Palace
  Court, Bayswater Road, London W2 4LP.
India: The Counsellor (Science and Education), The High
  Commission of India, India House, Aldwych, London WC2B 4NA.
Luxembourg: The Luxembourg Ambassador, Luxembourg Embassy,
  27 Wilton Crescent, London SW1X 8SD.
Thailand: The Education Counsellor, Thai Government Students
  Office, The Royal Thai Embassy, 28 Princes Gate, London SW7 1GF.

Studying and Living in Britain - the British Council's Guide, Northcote
House Publishers, Plymbridge House, Estover Road, Plymouth PL6 7PZ.

Student Life

Student Life: A Survival Guide by Natasha Roe, published by Hobsons
Publishing.

And some further addresses

The Association of Recognised English Language Services (ARELS), 2
Pontypool Place, London SE1 8QF; Tel: 0171 242 3136.

British Council, Information Centre, 10 Spring Gardens, London SW1A
2BN; Tel: 44 161 957 7755.

The British Tourist Authority, 12 Regent Street, London SW1Y 4PQ.

Heist, 2 College Close, Beckett Park Campus, Leeds LS6 3QS; Tel: 0113
226858.

CSU Limited, Armstrong House, Oxford Road, Manchester M1 7ED;
Tel: 0161 236 9816.

National Association Recognition Information Centre, British Council,
Medlock Street, Manchester M15 4AA.

The Open University, Walton Hall, Milton Keynes, MK7 6AA; Tel:
01908 274066.

The POSTGRAD Series, available on the Net at http://www.hob-sons.co.uk

SKILL: National Bureau for Students with Disabilities, 336 Brixton Road, London SW9 7AA; Tel: 0171 274 0565.

Social Work Admissions System, Fulton House, Jessop Avenue, Cheltenham, Gloucestershire GL50 3SH; Tel: 01242 225977.

UCAS, Fulton House, Jessop Avenue, Cheltenham, Gloucester GL50 3SH; Tel: 01242 227788 (general enquiries).

UKCOSA: The Council for International Education – a registered charity which provides information, advice and training about the recruitment, support and education of international students. It responds to queries from prospective students world-wide and will also advise on topics like immigration, employment law, financial aid and fees and grants. Contact UKCOSA at 9–17 St Albans Place, London N1 0NX; Tel: 0171 354 5210.

University of London External Scheme, University of London, Senate House, Malet Street, London EC1E 7HU.

Index

173

See also the Glossary, pages 155–164

Also published by Kogan Page…

Choosing a university? This volume is updated annually:

University Places 1997, 3rd edition

**While at university, these guides will help you
to study successfully:**

The Student's Guide to Passing Exams, Richard Burns
The Student's Guide to Preparing Dissertations and Theses, Brian Allison
The Student's Guide to Writing Essays, David Roberts

**Other titles will help you to choose your future career and find a
job after university:**

A–Z of Careers and Jobs, 8th edition, Diane Burston
How to Pass Graduate Recruitment Tests, Mike Bryon
How to Pass Numeracy Tests, Harry Tolley and Ken Thomas
How to Pass Selection Tests, Mike Bryon and Sanjay Modha
How to Pass Technical Selection Tests, Mike Bryon and Sanjay Modha
How to Pass the Civil Service Qualifying Tests, Mike Bryon
How to Pass Verbal Reasoning Tests, Harry Tolley and Ken Thomas
How You Can Get That Job! Application Forms and Letters Made Easy,
     Rebecca Corfield
The Job Hunter's Handbook, David Greenwood
Job Hunting After University or College, Jan Perrett
Job Hunting Made Easy: A Step-by-Step Guide, 3rd edition, John
     Bramham and David Cox
Manage Your Own Career, Ben Bell
Offbeat Careers: 60 Ways to Avoid Becoming an Accountant, 3rd edition,
     Vivien Donald
Preparing Your Own CV, Rebecca Corfield
Readymade CVs, Lynn Williams
Readymade Job Search Letters, Lynn Williams
Test Your Own Aptitude, 2nd edition, Jim Barrett and Geoff Williams
Working for Yourself: The Daily Telegraph Guide to Self-Employment,
     17th edition, Godfrey Golzen

Learn how to study better, not harder!

If you want to go to university, you have to make sure you get the right marks. Even dropping one grade can make the difference between your first and second choice. Just published, The How to Study Series has been written to help you to make the most of precious study time – however little you may have left! Each book helps you plan, organise and excel at studying so that neither you nor your social life suffer too much.

How to Study

This book starts by helping you to look at whether you are making the best of your study time – and then shows you how to do your best even when time is short.

£8.99 ISBN: 0 7494 2351 X
186 pages 1997 Order no: KT351

Last Minute Study Tips

This guide is full of tips and techniques to help you succeed – whether your deadline is months, weeks, days, or merely hours and minutes away.

£6.99 ISBN: 0 7494 2345 5
108 pages 1997 Order no KT345

Improve Your Reading

Reading and digesting information (often quite quickly) is a key part of studying. This guide will help you get to the information you want – and use it effectively in your studies.

£6.99 ISBN: 0 7494 2348 X
92 pages 1997 Order no: KT348

Improve Your Writing

This guide shows how by following a few simple rules any student can improve the structure and style of an essay or dissertation – and gain better marks.

£6.99 ISBN: 0 7494 2347 1
92 pages 1997 Order no: KT347

Improve Your Memory

You can improve your memory for anything – dates, facts, even spelling. This book shows you how.

£6.99 ISBN: 0 7494 2349 8
92 pages 1997 Order no: KT349

Getting Organised

If you're just starting to feel the pressure of looming exams, you need this book. It contains everything you need to set up a personal organisation system that really works.

£6.99 ISBN: 0 7494 2346 3
92 pages 1997 Order no: KT346

These books by Ron Fry have helped millions of people to study better, and to achieve better results. In these new editions of his successful 'How to Study' programme, you can learn the proven techniques and tips to improve your own learning.

Coming Soon: **Pass Any Test, Use Your Computer, Take Notes,** and **Manage Your Time.** Available from all good bookshops or directly from the address below.

Kogan Page Ltd, 120 Pentonville Road, London N1 9JN Tel: 0171 278 0545 Fax: 0171 278 8198

e-mail: kpinfo @ kogan-page.co.uk